Talent Isn't Enough

**Ten Ways to Enhance Your Chances of Acting
Success and Build the Winner's Mindset**

Charlotte Thornton

ISBN-13: 978-1-9767717-9-8

Is there anything I could say that would put you off becoming an actor?

What if I said it might take ten years?

What if I said others, less talented than you, will find success before you?

That many of those successful actors won't work as hard as you or be as nice?

What if I told you the path would be unfair, non-linear and full of frustrations?

Would that put you off beginning?

If so, put this book down.

If not, then turn the page...

Table of Contents

Introduction

Who is this book for?

This book is for drama school graduates just starting out on their journey, more experienced actors who have been working hard but getting nowhere, or those who are semi-established in the acting industry, but not where they would like to be. In fact, anyone in the performing arts with a goal can use the tools in this book.

Why read this book?

If your career were going the way you wanted it to, you wouldn't be looking at this book. You've chosen it because you are looking for the answers, tools and strategies to succeed. This book will offer you those tools. Tools you can use whatever level you are at.

If you want to get fit you can start going to the gym. If you are an athlete wanting to reach peak fitness (whilst staying uninjured) you get a trainer or a coach. The same is true for any goal, we can do a lot alone, but with a coach we can get further, faster. As an actor you have chosen one of the most rewarding careers, but also one of the most competitive and challenging. If you want to cut your learning time and turbo-charge your career you need a mentor: a coach. I am that coach; this book is my coaching.

It took eight years before I found my coach, but the impact of having one was seen in far less time. I went to LA in my thirties, an agentless actor struggling on the fringes without a mentor, an effective plan or any real contacts. Within a year of working with a coach, I had an agent and my first equity contract. Two years after that, I was making my West End Debut.

Before then, I had worked very hard for years, trying to get doors to open and trying to be seen. I was proactive, diligent and I worked on my craft. Yet I was stuck, without even an agent for years. In desperation I devoured innumerable business success books and personal development books. I learnt some helpful things that I have included in this guide but largely the business books did not apply to the business of acting. This book does.

When I graduated from drama school I didn't get an agent. I was devastated. I didn't know what to do next. There were no acting coaches that I could find and no one I knew had walked the path before me. I had no mentor, no contacts and no agent. I wish I had known twenty years ago what I know now. I had to make it up as I went along and learn by failing. But *you* don't have to. You can get the advice, ideas and strategies here in this book, for less than the cost of a large glass of wine.

Why should you listen to me?

Good question. Clearly, you can't take the advice of just anyone. So, who am I? I am an actor who has learned and applied these tools and used them to take me from dead end to the West End. In addition, I have been on all sides of the table. I have been actor, agent and casting assistant. I have a 360-degree picture of the industry. Only the UK has cooperative agencies, agencies run by actors, and they are a fantastic way to see what's going on in the business from the inside. I worked as an agent in a cooperative agency for five years.[1] When I was in LA I worked as an intern in the office of an Oscar winning casting director. I read film scripts, did day-to-day admin, and I was in charge of running the camera in the castings. I watched audition after audition and was involved in the feedback each actor got.

I have also worked in Public Relations (PR). PR is partly about making relationships with the media, but mainly it is about getting your brand out in front of the right audience enough times for it to have impact. It is about being known and trusted. It's no good being brilliant if no one knows you exist. I will cover PR and marketing in this guidebook, so you can run your business as a business. I have included a whole chapter on leveraging social media, because I think this is a powerful and empowering medium that anyone can utilise – irrespective of status, contacts or wealth.

In addition to what I learned as an actor, agent, casting assistant and in PR, I also include ideas from my own coach – the amazing Dallas Travers. I met Dallas in LA and she changed how I had been working. Lessons I had learnt but not yet processed suddenly became obvious. Now I had a guide, someone on my team. It cut my learning time in half. My mindset started to change first, and then my behaviour and actions aligned with my new thinking. In a few years I went from an unrepresented actor working day jobs and performing profit-share theatre to having a role on the West End. It didn't happen overnight, but it did happen.

This was not just the result of perseverance, though that was a factor, it was the result of a giant shift in my marketing strategy, in my inner belief systems, and my approach. This is what I believe I can teach you – whoever you are, connected or not, represented or not, beautiful, quirky or just plain normal.

---

[1] The first agent I got after my eight years flying solo was a cooperative agency, which is an agency run by actors. It is a fantastic way to learn about the industry because you're being an agent each week, submitting other actors for work, reading breakdowns and calling casting directors. There is also a wonderful support network of the other actors, though these types of agencies still receive some stigma within the industry simply because they're run by actors.

Smooth seas do not make skilled sailors

Success is not always the best teacher, because success doesn't necessarily correlate to having used a successful strategy. Some actors succeed purely because they are lucky. That is not a strategy, so it can't be taught. The reality is that – in spite of how much we as a society like to think success is just hard work and talent – many successful actors have had the good fortune to be fast tracked by luck, beauty or connections.

By connections I mean anything from being born into the right family or being represented by a powerful agent. The former can guide you in your career choices and introduce you to the right people, a good agent can open doors or insist you are seen (leveraging their connections to high profile actors).[2] Training at the Royal Academy of Dramatic Arts (RADA), a drama school whose reputation alone gives an actor credibility, may also open doors for the graduate actor.

I am not suggesting that these actors haven't worked hard or that they are undeserving. Simply that if the rise to success is the result of factors outside of the actors' control, then this cannot be taught. For example, if I were the daughter of a big star, a director or producer might hire me knowing my name would have a draw for audiences. Or s/he might meet me for a casting out of curiosity. These opportunities might be the beginning of a successful acting career, but I wouldn't be able to teach you <u>how</u> I'd become successful.

You cannot be taught how to open doors by people who had doors opened for them. And without an audition, no matter how talented you might be, you could slip through the net. Sadly, this happens to many good actors, who either never make it or get so frustrated that they quit. That is why it is so important, as well as working on your craft, to have some strategies that will get you through the door and help you to leave a good and lasting impression when you do. These strategies are in this book.

Turbo-Charge your Career

I am passionate about personal development, coaching and mentoring. I want you to succeed. And simply put, I believe that if you follow these strategies, then you will substantially enhance your chances.

If nothing else, I hope my story motivates you to hang in there that little while longer, and to find success in whatever outcomes occur. Because there are no guarantees to being talented, or hard working, sometimes luck is required. You can't learn luck, but you can learn everything else.

By the end of this book you will know:

---

[2] If a production wants a famous actor for their show, the agent could also request (in exchange) that the production casts some of the agency's lesser-known actors in smaller roles.

- How the industry works
- How to make those important career decisions
- What your goals are and how to set them
- What is blocking your success and what to do about it
- An action plan of what to do with timelines and bite-size steps
- What your brand is and how to sell it
- How to use social media to market your career
- How to feel confident and happy whichever route your career takes

Disclaimer: This is not the truth (no book is)

I don't know everything. I have my own experience, ideas, research, but I am not omniscient. You should probably be wary of any 'expert' that says that they know everything or who states that there is one truth. This is not the answer to *all* your challenges. It is a guide: a collection of lessons, tools, thoughts, and learnings.

You're already on the road; I am just showing you some shortcuts. I took the long way and I'm back to tell you how to avoid unnecessary detours. So read the book, but remember it is one person's experience and opinion (with a few others referenced along the way). Take responsibility for your own decisions and your own path. Therein your true power lies.

Thank you and good luck on your journey! Charlotte

Strategy One – Give up the fight

It is likely that this is not the strategy you were expecting to find at the beginning of this book. It might seem strange for a motivational book to start with the words *give up the fight*, but it is because this seems counter intuitive that we need to address it first. Having fire and passion is great. Fighting is not. Fighting implies that there is an enemy. It is aggressive and desperate. Fighting is what we do when our lives depend on something. You may feel your life depends upon being an actor. I understand that passion. I have felt that way. But the *fight* could be holding you back.

I spent eight years without an agent, representing myself, struggling to be seen and wasting time in mundane day jobs to pay my rent. But I never gave up fighting. I decided that I'd carry on for as long as it took. I would just work harder and harder. I never set an age - 'make it by 30 or else give up'. There was no point in setting an end date because I knew that acting was all I wanted to do.

But I was getting knocked down. My struggle mentality and my strategy to *just keep fighting* were exhausting me, and more importantly, they weren't working. Ironically, it was when I decided to quit acting at 35 years old, 11 years after drama school, that things really started to happen for me. I never thought I would quit; yet this was the making of me.

At 34 I had tried everything. My pre-agent years (all eight of them) revolved around fringe theatre, low budget films and tours of old people's homes. I had performed Shakespeare, Cabaret and Improv. I had written and performed my own stand up, had a personal trainer and gone to LA (twice). I had changed my hair colour. Not only was I <u>not</u> on the path to success, I couldn't see that a path existed for people like me at all.

Success seemed to exist purely for those lucky, well connected, and represented actors. Those who seemed (in my eyes) to have it easy. My optimism and hope were being slowly eaten away and replaced with anger and bitterness. Not an attractive energy to be carrying around but I was too absorbed in the unfairness of it to even notice.

My low point came after a particularly pointless audition; the script was at best unfunny and at worst, offensive. The producer pretended the read-through was a recall so he didn't have to pay the cast to hear his play read. Then a phone call from one of our agents revealed the theatre didn't even have the show scheduled to run there. The whole thing had been a giant waste of time, a farce.

I finally decided I'd had enough. It had been 10 years since I'd left drama school, and though I didn't know what else I would do, I just knew I couldn't do this anymore. I wrote my mum an email saying, "I hope you are not disappointed in me, but I cannot see a way. I've tried everything." But as they say about low points – the darkest hour is before the dawn.

I was still a member of Equity (the British actors' union) and Spotlight (an online casting site) so I thought I would wait until these memberships expired, then I would tell my agent I was quitting. I decided to do one last mail out, to send out all my remaining headshots so that I had nothing left, nothing wasted, when I had quit.

This is when my professional career really began. When I ceased to grasp so tightly and let go, a miracle happened. I got two auditions for established paid productions: one through my agent and one through my last-chance mailing. I attended both. I got recalled for the first play but I didn't attend because by then I'd accepted the second play, which was my first job on the West End.

This is the power of surrendering.

Wanting something too much comes across as desperate. We don't seem ambitious we seem pushy, controlling and needy. If you have ever dated a pushy, controlling or needy person you will know that it is a turn off. In the very same way, work relationships can also be turned off by this attitude and energy. It repels rather than attracts. The strategy you want is one of detachment, acceptance and happiness.

Detachment

Detachment can sound impossible to the passionate – *this is all I've ever dreamed of doing with my life* – actor. I am not saying it is easy, but it is possible and it is necessary. Buddhists believe that it is our attachment to things that causes suffering, rather than the things themselves. Detachment, for actors, is about fully committing to and believing the role is yours, but knowing that you will be okay whether you get it or not.

Detachment connects to the other attitudes of acceptance and happiness. When we are at peace with ourselves, and the world, we can accept whichever outcome and still be happy. As well as ensuring you are content, whether you get the part or not, happiness can help you get your goal because it makes you attractive. Not in a literal physical way, though actually that too, but in the magnetic sense of the word. People want to spend time and work with, happy, positive people. Struggling and being desperate will create an unattractive energy that will repel contacts and work opportunities. The solution is to be happy.

In his book, *The Happiness Advantage*, Shawn Achor writes, "More than a decade of ground-breaking research in the fields of positive psychology and neuroscience has proven in no uncertain terms that the relationship between success and happiness works the other way around...happiness is the precursor to success, not merely the result." He adds that, "happiness and optimism actually fuel performance and achievement – giving us the competitive edge".

Stop thinking of yourself as a fighter, and start to see yourself as an athlete. You work hard, you train and you have a holistic approach. You know you must compete but you're more concerned with beating your own personal best than fighting external forces. As an actor this translates to getting good at your craft, being focused, determined, disciplined and setting achievable goals. But being too attached to a goal is as dangerous as not having one. We need to have a goal, but not have our happiness dependent upon the attainment of it. We need to be happy regardless. This is what Vishen Lakhiani, founder of Mindvalley, calls the paradox of intention and it is a paradox: we must want it, but not too much.

I used to believe that if you were happy now, then what would be your motivation to change and move forward? If you're happy now, as things are, then surely that's where you will stay. Not so. That is the place from which to build your dream and vision. You can't build those from a place of unhappiness.

Let me give you an example. As a single gal in my twenties, I went to a trendy Clapham bar with two girlfriends. We saw three hot guys. Unfortunately, all the other gorgeous Clapham girls had spied them too. After attempts to vie for their attention, probably pouting or doing whatever we thought was alluring, we decided we couldn't be bothered wasting our time competing with the other girls. We gave up trying to get the guys' attention and decided just to have a laugh.

We started dancing for fun, which led into a silly dance off with the moves getting more and more ridiculous. We weren't being sexy at all. Yet, the guys came over to buy us drinks saying that it was the funniest thing they'd seen. We got the guys because we gave up trying. They were attracted not by the game playing of us not trying (it hadn't been a game plan at all) but by the fact that we looked like the most fun girls to hang out with that night and they wanted a fun night.

I believe my acting success also occurred when I let go, because I became less desperate and less needy. I had detached from the outcome. I had accepted myself – successful or not. I also believe I empowered myself by quitting the part of the acting business that didn't align with my values: the part that sucked. The part that, perhaps more significantly, was not making me happy. In *Strategy Three* we will look at this further in the Power of Saying No! But first, let's look at, and destroy, the first of many cultural myths: the myth that all you need to do is work hard.

The myth of hard work

If you fail for a sustained period of time, despite working hard, then it makes sense to question the fundamental principles and beliefs upon which you are acting. Somewhere something is going wrong. If you are failing it makes sense to look at your recipe for success. Do you have the right ingredients? I believed the ingredients for success were talent, hard work and perseverance. I was working hard, I believed I was talented and I had paid my dues year after year after year and yet, in terms of making a living as an actor, I hadn't got anywhere.

In my moments of self-doubt, where I wondered if I was actually talented enough, I reminded myself that bad actors worked all the time. I could see them on TV (and/or) at the theatre. I also saw many good actors slipping through the net. So, I decided that even though I wasn't successful this was not due to lack of talent. But sadly, talent isn't enough. As for the other ingredients, hard work and perseverance, I was doing these. So what was going wrong? It never occurred to me that the formula I was taught (talent+ hard work +perseverance = success) might be flawed. I am here to tell you that it is.

I don't know about you but I was always told that success was a product of hard work. I received a message from my parents and my culture that: if you want success you must work hard. Fact. In fact, you must do more that just work hard, you must struggle and fight. Perseverance, struggle and sacrifice, this is what it took. The myth I'd like to break here and now is this: *success is the result of hard work, and hard work will eventually bring you success.* Not necessarily true!

In his book, *The Slight Edge,* Jeff Olson writes "I knew that the only way I could ever become anybody was by working hard and being persistent....I didn't know it yet, but just working harder doesn't do it. If it did, then everyone who works hard would have made it. All you have to do is look around you and you can see that this isn't the case. The world is chock full of people who are working their butts off – and still getting their butts kicked by circumstance."

This hard work myth is easy to believe, partly because it's ingrained in us from a young age, like the tooth fairy or Santa Claus, but mainly because it seems plausible and logical. What is more logical than believing that input (your effort) and output (your achievements) are connected? And in some cases this can be true. If we take something that is essentially scientific, like improving your fitness, then the more work you put in the more calories you burn, the more likely you are to improve your muscle tone. On the whole, in fitness, input and output are connected. Your hard work is rewarded. But don't make the mistake of thinking that this rule applies to all areas of your life. It doesn't.

10

Think of the fly buzzing against the windowpane. It is desperate to get out, but it doesn't understand the concept of glass. It seems convinced that the solution is to persist. Next to the pane of glass is an open window, but the fly just tries and tries again. No matter how much hard work (or positive thinking) the fly is doomed to fail unless it changes strategy. More hard work is NOT the solution; it is the death of the fly.

Taking responsibility

My family is originally from Yorkshire, a county in the North of England. For those of you unfamiliar with Yorkshire, embedded in the culture is what Yorkshire folk call *graft*. Graft is Yorkshire speak for hard work. Hard work was instilled in me as both right and honourable, the true and only path to success.

This work ethic, not exclusive to Yorkshire I'm sure, has impacted on many others and me. I worked three different jobs at one point, six days a week, giving them my all, whilst also trying to pursue my acting career, see friends and family and do life admin (cleaning, laundry etc.). I used to boast about how long it had been since my last day off. In some ways it protected me from judgement. Whilst I was so clearly working my socks off, no one could point the finger at me, as the reason to why I was failing. I could evade responsibility even if I wasn't where I wanted to be.

I am sure there are people who have to work even harder than me. People who clean offices at night and then do other physical jobs during the day. People in the third world who walk miles for clean water. I am not, for one moment, saying I had it desperately hard. I am saying my ethos was, as long as I worked hard, the failure was not mine but the world's, for being unfair.

It made me feel bitter, that I was working hard and not seeing results, but also it made me not take responsibility for *how* I was working. The blame lay with the unfair world – I was doing my part. I knew I was doing my part because I worked most days and was exhausted. Not only did my acting career suffer, but also my health suffered. Instead of getting lots of acting opportunities I got really ill. It was my body's way of saying, "Stop – this isn't working".

The fight we need to surrender is the constant fight to be perfect, to push, control and make things happen. The more we push the more resistance we meet. Do not push. Be prepared, proactive, well researched but never pushy. I'll talk more about this when we get onto marketing but, for example, a proactive person writes a passionate, specific letter to the director of a show they love and are right for. A pushy person does repeated, generalised mailings of 100 or so letters, because they think input and output are related, and if they could just write more letters then there would be more auditions and more work.

11

This relies on the old myth, on life being fair, on a belief that eventually something will stick. My personal experience is that this isn't just a numbers game. We can be cleverer than that. If you want to play a numbers game, get a lottery ticket. If you have a mentality of perfectionism and overworking, I urge you to stop and take stock.

Secondly, the fight can make us angry and bitter. We want the world to be fair, for input and output to be related, because then we can just work harder to get the results. But when the results don't arrive we get angry. We don't understand. We followed the rule. We worked hard. We struggled. Why don't we have what we deserve?

I've complained to others and myself many a time, "but I'm working harder than anyone else". I believed I was. The point was it doesn't matter. I was working ridiculously hard but output and input aren't necessarily related. And sadly life isn't fair. So we can moan about it, spread bad energy and get even less for our hard work, or we can accept it and use it to our advantage.

The day this lesson really came home to me was when I finished a video shoot for a well-known pharmaceutical brand. I worked a four-hour day and was paid somewhere around £2,000 (about $3,000). It was the largest amount of money I'd earned in one day before, let alone one half day. In addition, it had been fun and easy.

I suddenly realised how strange that was. How could I have earned so much money so easily if output and input were related? Surely £2,000 would be harder to earn in four hours than the £62.50 earned in the same time on a basic theatre contract, or the four-hour wage of a waiter or office assistant. But no, it had been easier. That's when it clicked for me. They are not related. And the more I thought about it the more I realised that the people earning the most amount of money were not necessarily working or fighting harder.

I was elated. Why? Because now I could stop working so hard. I could stop making myself ill, stop making myself bitter and live a more fulfilled, easier and more successful life.

Now, I am not suggesting that we do nothing or that you should be lazy. I think you should be conscientious, learn your lines, be on time, be prepared, do your research, make goals and plans to achieve them. I am saying that there is a way of working that is laser-focused and effective, and a way of working that is just hard. Stop doing the latter and start doing the former.

If you are the kind of actor who does nothing and just lets your agent do all the work, then I'm not talking to you at this point. This is a chapter for people who are working too hard in the wrong areas: the strugglers, the pushers, the perfectionists. You will know if this is you because you are trying everything and failing, you are exhausted.

There is work to be done, but it is not the fighting I was taught to do. It's more intelligent than that and it involves personal growth. It's work that isn't about the hours you put in but the risks you take, the struggles you overcome not the ones you continue to live. I learned how to work smarter instead of harder.

The amount of hours, the amount of stress, the amount of pushing does not equate to the number of auditions or jobs you will secure. As coach Tony Robinson says, "Running east looking for a sunset, I don't care how positive you are, I don't care how hard you work at it, it's not going to work, it's the wrong strategy."

There is however, a caveat. When it comes to becoming a better actor, a more skilled actor, let's say a more talented one, then there is a connection between input and output. In his book *Outliers*, Malcolm Gladwell studies successful people in a variety of industries from music to IT and demonstrates that the talented have all worked at their craft for 10,000 hours.

10,000 hours is what it takes to be the best, to be what he describes as extraordinarily talented. Talent is about hard work. But he also shows that the ones who turn 'being the best' into legendary success also had extraordinary opportunities. Gladwell says, "...what truly distinguishes their histories is not their extraordinary talent, but their extraordinary opportunities...Their success is not exceptional or mysterious. It is grounded in a web of advantages and inheritances, some deserved, some not, some earned, some plain lucky – but all critical to making them who they are. The outlier, in the end, is not an outlier at all."

So, what does this mean? That it's all down to luck, we should just give up? Yes and no. If you are put off by the challenge, by the fact that this journey is unlikely to be fair, straightforward, or easy – then by all means make another choice. But if you won't be put off, if you want to give it a shot against the odds, and you want to try and play the cards you've been dealt to the best possible level you can, then read on. Let's do everything we can to earn and create those extraordinary opportunities. There's a quote attributed to various different people, which says, "When the dream is big enough, the facts don't matter."

So, we need to separate the craft from the business. The craft takes 10,000 hours; you must work hard and do the work. Leveraging that talent to make a career from it is another task entirely, and it is that part, where I am suggesting we work smarter, not harder. This is where I ask you to give up the fight.

Most personal development books will tell you that if you want something different, do something different. So even if you haven't quite bought into destroying this myth just yet, I propose you try it. Experiment for a year doing things differently. You can only get different results and so either way you'll learn something. So, repeat after me: *input does not necessarily correlate to output*. How do we work smarter rather than harder? By using the strategies in this book.

Summary of lessons learnt

- Fighting seems admirable, yet it causes exhaustion and overworking
- Build your vision from a happy, contented space, not an unhappy one
- Being pushy, bitter and desperate are unattractive qualities that will repel opportunities
- Input and output are not always related
- Hard work is no guarantee of success
- The solution is not to stop working, but to work smarter
- Blaming the outside world stops us discovering what <u>we</u> can do to change the situation
- Separate the craft from the business
- Talent occurs after 10,000 hours work on your craft
- Talent alone is not enough

Strategy Two – Abandon false goals

The corporate world is often mocked for insisting goals be SMART. Which means Specific, Measurable, Achievable, Realistic and Timebound. But actually, this is a really useful mnemonic to assess our goals and ensure they are achievable. Setting up a goal that is unachievable will make you feel like a failure and impact your success journey.

How do we know if a goal is achievable though? Sometimes it can be a matter of opinion or perspective. Let's face it, as actors, we have all met those people who think our dreams are not achievable. For our purpose, I would like to set this definition. Achievable, means you can achieve it with a 100% certainty. If you cannot guarantee whether it is achievable or not, it is not a goal, but an objective or a vision. It might seem like I'm splitting hairs, but the difference is crucial and here it is:

A dream is something you want, a goal is something you can actually achieve.

This is not to say that you won't also achieve the dream. I am simply stating that a dream is a desire that cannot be achieved by you alone: other people and other factors are needed to create it. Goals, on the other hand, must be 100% within your control. Completing these goals will take you toward your dream making its attainment more likely.

Each year, in January, I would write out my New Year's resolutions, which essentially were my goals for the year. I had read that there was a powerful correlation between the 1% of people who have and write down goals, and the top performing 1%. I wanted to be in that top 1%. I had goals for each sector of my life: health, career, relationship, finance and growth.

Whilst most of my goals were achievable goals, my career goals were not goals at all. They were dreams. Why? Because they required action by others; actions that I could not control nor guarantee.

What I believed were my goals were things such as 'get an agent' and 'get a TV audition'. Each year I would try and achieve these goals, but I would fail because the agents and TV casting directors didn't respond. I couldn't control what action they took and yet, without them, I failed. The next year I would transfer across from the previous year any unfulfilled goals. Year after year I wrote 'get an agent' and 'get a TV audition' again. Every year I tried my best but I couldn't make it happen. As you can imagine this was totally demoralising, disempowering and disheartening. I felt like a failure.

The sad fact was that, despite working hard and struggling hard (which we've now addressed!) the goals 'get an agent' and 'get a TV audition' remained on that list, for over eight years. Eight years! Why? Because they weren't goals they were objectives and dreams that relied on other people to fulfil them.

I could not force someone to give me a TV audition or to represent me. So the 'goals' were unachievable by me. They were still things I wanted and needed to focus on, but by thinking of them as goals, I missed creating achievable goals for myself and got caught in a failure trap.

Conversely, my fitness goals for 2009 included: 'run the London marathon'. As long as I trained properly, with time to pace myself up from one mile to 18 (you don't run the full distance until the day), with good nutrition and sensible rest times, then this was an achievable goal. **Achievable by me.** That is the difference. That goal didn't rely on anyone else but me. It was within my power, because it was my choice to get up and run on an allocated day, or hit the snooze and stay in bed.

"When you establish a goal for yourself, ask yourself if you can personally initiate the outcome or not," writes Justina Vail in her book, *How to be a Happy Actor in a Challenging Business*. "Remember that you cannot control what other people do or feel... Make your goal something that has you in the driver's seat, and that you can, at least, initiate!"

Figure 1.

If you have 'goals' that you cannot actually achieve -100% through your choices and actions – then these are not goals they're objectives and visions. They are useful because we will use our objectives and visions to work back to the smaller achievable goals to take us there. But we want to judge our success in terms of our goals alone, and use the vision as inspiration (see Figure 1.)

Why have goals?

We need a direction otherwise we are aimless and vague, rather than focused and specific. Wanting to be an actor isn't enough. To achieve it, to *live the dream* we need some objectives: steps that will take you where you want to go. The one-mile, ten-mile, sixteen-mile programme that will set you up for the metaphorical marathon. We also need a detailed plan of goals that help us achieve those objectives. Having goals we can achieve and do achieve makes us feel successful and feeling successful helps us develop the winner's mindset: a mindset that is programmed for success.

Vision

Let's start with your vision. I am using this word instead of dream, because dream has a quality of unattainability to it. A vision turns 'the dream' into an inspiring image of our future. The vision is the overall destination. It is like Stanislavski's concept of the Super Objective – a character's overall desire through the play. Your vision defines where you want to go and how you want your life to be.

In a play, this super objective is broken down to smaller objectives scene-by-scene, and then to line-by-line intentions of the character. In our personal development work, we will gradually break the vision down into objectives and then goals. The vision is the super objective; the goals are the smaller pieces that build towards it.

So, what is your vision? Is it about the stage or the screen, or a life of both? Is it about being respected or famous, wealthy or being an actor who takes great risks and does a wealth of varied roles. Not everyone's acting vision looks the same. What does yours look like?

Close your eyes and imagine yourself five years from now. You are writing me a letter that says, "Dear Charlotte, it has been five years since I read your book, but wow what a five years they've been. I have had the best five years of my career, let me tell you what has happened...". What follows? What do you write next? This is the vision. It doesn't need to be achievable by you, alone, at this stage, so think big.

Get specific

The more specific you are about your vision the more likely you are to achieve it. To get clear about what you want and what's important to you, take some quiet time to consider and answer these questions.

- What would you do if you knew you couldn't fail?

- What would you do if money were no object?

- Who do you envy? We often see envy as a bad thing, but it can indicate to us what we truly desire. If you can look at those you envy and think, "I want that for me", instead of feeling something negative about those you envy, then it can bring real clarity

- Why do you want to be an actor? Knowing your <u>why</u> can help you discover further levels of meaning, purpose and motivation

The more excited you are about the vision the better, because excitement is our source of inspiration. Firstly, it'll make you more passionate, which is contagious and feels genuine when you write to people. Plus, the more excited you are about something the more you know you are on the right path, and consequently, the more likely you are to take the necessary action.

Now you know where you want to go, you must look at where you are now and build the stepping-stones towards it. We will use achievable goals and objectives to create a plan.

For example:

Vision – I want to work as an actor on TV dramas, doing a variety of different programmes.
Where am I now – I have never had a TV part, not even a one liner.
Steps in between (Objectives) – Get a one-line part, get a medium part, and get a bigger part.
NB: None of these are goals yet. How do we know? Because we haven't yet got down to something achievable by the actor.

Objectives

What would you like to achieve in your career next? It might be a specific credit you'd like on your résumé. It might be to build a relationship with a specific person: casting director, producer or writer. Ask yourself, if you could wave a magic wand, what would the next phone call bring you? If you're thinking, *I'd like to be a Hollywood star*, that's too vague and more like a vision. It's not the specific next step.

Imagine the phone rings and your agent says, "They want to see you for...." Or "you've just booked the role of..." What? What have they told you? Does this objective fit into your bigger vision? Will it take you there? Continue thinking and visualising what it feels like to have that next career step happen for you. Then write it down. This is the objective that we will be using to create our goals from.

Time line

Next, when do you want to achieve this objective by? This may seem like an odd question. When I first heard it at a coaching seminar, my internal voice was saying, "Yesterday, I'd like to have achieved this yesterday, I'm years behind". Then I realised this was counterproductive. I can't set a goal in the past or else I'll never achieve it. But I felt, as you might at times, that I was behind. I hadn't had an agent for eight years of my career, and it felt as if I was playing catch up. If this is you, I discuss 'making comparisons' more in the final strategy on building emotional resilience.

Back to our specific objective. Pick a date in the future, when you'd like to achieve this objective by. Now we're going to do a couple of exercises with it. If you think your objective or ideal timescale is unrealistic, write it down anyway, we'll work on it.

Write a present tense statement dated in the future which states that the objective has already been achieved. If my objective were to get a decent sized role in a high profile, highly regarded television drama and I would like to achieve this in the next two months, I would write:

- It is now 13th March 20XX and I have a decent sized role in a high profile, highly regarded television drama.

- I might want to get even more specific and name the show. It is now February 2020 and I have a part on Line of Duty.

Believe to achieve

Take the above statement and, if you have a willing partner, then look them in the eye and repeat this phrase to them over and over for three minutes non-stop. Instil this phrase with a sense of belief. Believing is the first step to achieving but sometimes it's hard to believe straight away. We need to work the belief into our mind and our senses.

Luckily, you're an actor, so you can fake it until you make it. You will find that by the end of the exercise you believe this statement more than you did at the beginning. Hold on to that, you will understand its importance as the book progresses.

If you haven't got a willing partner use a mirror. But speak out loud and maintain eye contact. You might laugh (great!), you might feel silly (so what!), but you will finish the exercise believing it more than you did at the start. That is the purpose. Believing you can achieve what you want to achieve is crucial. Let me say that again. **Believing you can achieve what you want to achieve is crucial**.

If you don't believe it you won't achieve it. As Henry Ford said, "Whether you think you can or you think you can't, you're right". We act based on our thoughts and beliefs, so if we don't believe we can achieve something we won't take the right actions towards it.

To get our objective clear, carefully consider and answer the following questions. We have just covered 1 and 2.

- What do you want (objective)?

- By when (timeline)?

- How will you know that you have achieved it? What does success look like?

- What's the desired outcome of you achieving your objective?

- How will achieving it benefit you and/or others?

- What, if anything, have you already done to achieve your objective?

- What challenges have you met?

- Which ones did you overcome and how?

- Which obstacles remain or might arise?

Example

I answered the above for my dream to get a role on television, a few years ago. Here is what I wrote:

- What do you want? *To get a role on television*

- By when? *By November 2014*

- How will you know that you have achieved it? *I will be on set having hair and make-up done whilst running a few lines*

- What's the desired outcome of you achieving your objective? *A decent pay check, higher profile, more television experience, joy for me and those close to me who know I've waited a long time for it, the feeling of success*

- How will achieving it benefit me and/or others? *My confidence will improve, I will be happier, my family will be thrilled, and I might inspire others*

- What, if anything, have you already done to achieve your objective? *Gone to drama school, filmed a show reel, got an agent, written to television casting directors and attended their workshop/classes.*

- What challenges have you met? *Not being seen by any television casting directors except one. Challenge of nerves. Limited beliefs about my experience and my profile not being good enough.*

- Which ones did you overcome and how? *Worked on my limiting beliefs and gained more confidence through the workshops*

- Which obstacles remain or might arise? *I still need to get through the door. Be seen. Be known.*

Goals

We establish our goals by asking Question 10.

- What can I do to move me towards this objective?

Write down all the things you could do (100% actionable by you), to move towards this objective. Then brainstorm multiple ideas with the final question, which is: what else could you do? Ask your mind directly – what else could I do? Pause, take time to listen and hear what answers come through.

Keep asking yourself over and over. Write down any and all ideas without judgment. This isn't the time to judge but to expand and explore: practise lateral (creative) rather than vertical (logical) thinking. There are no rules. No bad ideas. Use your creative juices. If they're not flowing go out for a walk. Or get some friends round and see what ideas they come up with. Dismiss nothing.

You should now have a list of crazy options, normal options, and dull options. Ask yourself again what else could I do?

The author of *Think and Grow Rich*, Napoleon Hill, writes about his brainstorm method using his heroes: Emerson, Pain, Edison, Darwin, Lincoln, Burbank, Napoleon, Ford and Carnegie. He would call them to a cabinet meeting where he discussed his business challenges with them. He credits them with many ideas, instincts and hunches that came to him after these meetings.[3]

---

[3] "Every night, over a long period of years, I held an imaginary council meeting with this group whom I called my "Invisible Counselors" …while the members of my Cabinet may be purely fictional and the meetings existent only in my imagination…I can truthfully say that I owe entirely to my "Invisible Counselors" full credit for such ideas, facts or knowledge as I received through "inspiration"." Napoleon Hill, *Think and Grow Rich*.

Who is your hero or heroine? What would they do in your situation? What would your heroes advise you to do if they were here, at your brainstorm? Can you use this role playing tool, to generate further goals for your plan? The purpose here is to explore, and go further than the point at which you would normally stop.

Before I went to LA, I invested in a fitness trainer. I would give my all until the session was over, and then there'd be another exercise to do. I felt I had not saved energy for it. I thought I was spent, but I still had to do it. In these moments, you have to find it somewhere, you learn how to dig deep, and this is a really important skill for those wanting success, wanting an extraordinary life.

At the point where I had spent all my energy and was made to do more running or more weights, that's the stretch that made me stronger and fitter, not the 40 minutes prior to that which were in my comfort zone. So, do the same with your brain. Be patient with the gaps and the silences, it doesn't mean you're out of ideas yet. This is where you can push yourself. Be your own mental fitness trainer.

Keep asking past the point where you think/believe that you've come up with every idea possible. Sometimes when we hit resistance, it is because we fear the big idea. We pretend to be out of ideas, when we're not. We may think our mind is blank, it rarely is, and most likely we have censored ourselves unknowingly.

Ok, so you've felt uncomfortable and you have everything you could think of and then, found three more. Now look at these options and decide which will make it to your daily planner. Don't play safe. If you are after a dream job, and you are, you must, must, must be courageous.

You should now have some goals that you can achieve, which will take you towards your objective and ultimately your vision. List these goals out and schedule when you are going to action each and every one of them. If it's not scheduled it won't happen. Create a daily practice, like brushing your teeth, that ensures you are constantly and consistently moving towards your objective, via your goals.

In *The Slight Edge,* Jeff Olson, reiterates the idea of small, daily disciplines being more powerful than large, inconsistent action. We don't get fit from a one-off five-hour gym session, he argues. We get fit from exercising frequently. Habits are created by repetition, so daily disciplines will become habits, which eventually become automatic. Furthermore, daily discipline gets momentum going and sustains it. Random bursts, like the lift-off of a rocket, take more energy. So we only want to lift-off once and then move to maintaining momentum.

If you are disciplined you will take the required action. Olson states that, "Successful people do whatever it takes to get the job done, whether or not they feel like it". If your discipline is still a bit weak, then you could find someone to be your accountability partner. This is someone with whom you share your plan, your deadlines and then you check-in with them weekly to tell them your progress. You in turn can be their accountability partner for their goals. You want the results so you <u>must</u> take action. As personal development legend Jim Rohn once said, "If you really want something you'll find a way. If you don't, you'll find an excuse".

Power of Intention

When you work with your goals, objectives and visions, write them down. You might think, *I don't need to write it down - it's in my head*. But studies have shown a correlation between the writing of goals and the achievement of them. Writing it down is the simple part many overlook. It's not enough that you know the objective, you must make a statement of intent, and that includes writing your vision down, stating your objective out loud, telling people about it and putting your objective up somewhere you can see it.

The more visible it is, the more it will be in your mind daily. This reminds us to take daily steps toward that objective. These small steps accumulate and make a difference long term.

Blocks

Another way to prepare for success is to look at what might get in your way and find solutions ahead of time. Ask yourself what might stop you taking action? Look at these reasons; they will be a combination of obstacles and excuses. Obstacles we will find solutions for, excuses go into our list of limiting beliefs. So, which are which?

Let's imagine my vision is to be slim and healthy and my specific goal is to lose seven pounds by Christmas. My action plan may involve eating less and exercising more. If I then explain the challenges to this and say, "I find it hard because I have to walk past the bakery and it smells so good, I end up going in for croissants. Plus, I just don't have the time to exercise because I have kids and a job." The bakery is not a limiting belief it's an obstacle, quite literally, in the path of my slimming plan.

Solution to the obstacle might involve walking a different route, holding my nose past the bakery, ensuring I've already had breakfast before I walk past, or walking past as much as possible (perhaps with a buddy who stops me going in) to break the habit.

The story of not having time to exercise, because of my kids and my job is a limiting belief. I believe it to be true. I may even want it to be true because it ensures that I do not change. A part of me does not want to lose weight. It might be the goal of my conscious mind, but my unconscious mind believes it's safer for me not to change. The unconscious is clever. It provides what seem to be logical reasons. But these are limiting beliefs that need to be challenged and proved false, as we will discover in *Strategy Five*.

Celebrate success

Celebrate your successes and the achievement of any goals no matter how modest: from writing a letter to attending a workshop. Note any small successes and celebrate them. This will keep you positive and motivated, but more importantly, it creates a successful mindset. You start to see yourself as a successful person, and who you think you are is who you become.

Summary of lessons learnt

- A goal is something you can achieve
- When you dream, dream BIG, this is your vision
- Use objectives that will take you towards your vision
- Instil belief in the objective's attainment
- Write the objective down and ensure it is visible
- Brainstorm wild and wonderful goals
- Take action daily
- Celebrate and record your successes

Strategy Three – Say No!

This might, at first glance, seem another strange strategy, yet it has been one of the most powerful strategies I have ever learnt. Saying "No" is scary for actors. We think work leads to more opportunities and therefore to more work. Like the myth of hard work in *Strategy One*, it seems to be logical, but to say, "Yes" to anything and everything can be based on fear, on a 'lack' mentality.

We actors can over-busy ourselves out of fear. We fear being out of work, but fear should never be the place we take action from. Inspired action does not come from fear. Furthermore, these choices take us away from our true vision and expend our energy in the wrong direction.

My career coach, Dallas, teaches that our goal (or in our case our objective) is our compass. But in order to move toward it we must say No to anything taking us in another direction. Whilst we want to avoid being too attached to the outcome we are still going to be focused. We are not going to be diverted off course whatever tests come our way.

This means decluttering your schedule, taking out anything that is not in alignment with your objective, and saying No to offers that are going to detour you. This is the hard work! Sitting with the uncomfortable feeling of doing something new, of creating space for what we really want to manifest; the difficulty of having faith and believing in something before it has arrived – this is the hard work.

Sometimes saying Yes to everything seems appropriate. In my first year out of drama school, I decided I would say Yes to everything I got offered in order to get the most experience as quickly as possible. I hoped it would build momentum. This made sense because I didn't have an agent yet. But even in this year of saying Yes to everything, I turned a role down. I said No.

Bizarrely it was before I had learnt this rule but before I learned to mistrust my instincts. In this case, my gut instincts knew about saying No before I had the experience to understand that it is, not only safe, but also a really healthy and effective strategy.

As I explained, it was my first year out of drama school. I was living at home and waitressing at the restaurant at the end of my street. I was agentless so I had to find work myself though a few publications that pretty much only had unpaid, low paid or student productions in it.

It was in the days before the Internet (yes, there was such a time!) so it meant a lot of hard work writing letters and printing up résumés. I needed an agent to see me perform so I spent my time applying for fringe shows so I could invite agents to come. That was my strategy at the time. It was all I had.

I had decided that I would accept everything to get on the ladder and to learn. So, in a sense I had my compass, but then I went to an audition that left me feeling soulless. The audition was in a council flat in a shabby part of London. It was not run like a proper audition but more like the first read through you get once you have got the job. There were lots of us crammed into a small room, and the lady running the auditions (was she the writer, director, casting director, who knew?) didn't have enough copies of the text. So, being programmed to be keen and helpful, I offered to copy them and found myself in the local convenience store using the photocopy machine at about 8pm one night.

As I stood there at the copy machine, I thought, *this is ridiculous*. In my gut I just knew that someone who couldn't organise an audition properly would probably not be able to run rehearsals or produce a good quality show. How were they going to run a show if they couldn't run an audition? However, I got the copies done and went and read as best as I could.

I came home deflated and told my mum, "I'd rather be a waitress for the rest of my life". And there it was: my No; my boundary. This job was so bad I'd rather be a waitress. My mother told me that I didn't have to accept the job and that I was allowed to have standards. It was like a news flash. A light bulb went on. It hadn't occurred to me I could choose. They said beggars can't be choosers, I was agentless I was surely a beggar. Could I say No? It seemed arrogant, audacious.

But my mum was right. If I was going to do something I hated, I might as well carry on waitressing and at least get paid for it. The point seemed academic because I hadn't even been offered the job yet. They might not offer it to me. But I have since learnt that it's good to know - before the pressure is on, before you are put on the spot to make a decision - which way you are going to jump. I have also learnt how much success can come from pure audacity.

As it turns out, I was offered the job. I turned it down, much to their surprise. I then wrote a list of reasons why I would accept jobs in the future. It was a benchmark, if you like. I got really specific about money, exposure, what contacts it might create, the chance to stretch my skills as an actor and gain experience. Even details such as the show's location and the number of actors in the cast were factors, because I knew they would influence agent attendance.[4]

---

[4] Agents are more likely to come to a venue near where they work (central London, for example) and if they can see a lot of actors in one go, this too, is an incentive (as opposed to a one-man show).

I decided each job had to fulfil at least one of these criteria or else I would say No. As the years went on the list altered, but I always had a list of things that needed to be ticked off before I would say Yes! Think about your vision, what you want to achieve and write your own list of criteria. Then start saying No.

Saying No establishes your boundaries. When you have clear boundaries your goals become more focused and are therefore more achievable (see *Strategy Two*). Your energy is directed rather than dispersed. Saying No is simple, but it is not easy. It takes courage. Not everything that looks like an opportunity is one. We need to be able to tell the difference between an opportunity and a distraction, and have the courage to make mistakes.

If this sounds scary, let me reassure you that I have heard several stories of people turning down work and, each time, the directors and casting directors have respected them more for it. It has made them even keener to work with them another time, on another project.

If we take our dating analogy again, who wants to date the guy or girl who says Yes to anyone? Saying No tells people that we are discerning, that we know what we want and that we believe in ourselves enough to decline work that doesn't align with that vision. It is a position of power because we are the decision maker. It comes from a place of confidence, faith and security. (Not from a place of the demanding diva!)

When we ask for what we want, instead of just accepting whatever comes our way, we experience two things: a weird feeling of danger as we courageously jump and hope the net will appear, then surprise when the net actually appears. I have done this with acting work and with day jobs. I have said No and got more of what I really wanted in reward for my daring. Yes, you could drift from job to job with no goal, no plan, but I imagine that if you're reading this book it is because that either doesn't suit you or isn't working. So decide ahead what your criteria are based on your goals and objectives from the last chapter. Then you can judge work offers against your list, to see if they should be accepted or turned down.

Frequently the offers we need to turn down, because they're not in alignment with your goal or your values, don't sit right with us in the first place. We might have a gut feeling right from the start that the project isn't right for us, but we live in a society that values logic above instinct so we ignore this feeling. We need to do the opposite. To learn to tune in to this feeling and listen to what it is telling us.

I have, in the past, ignored my instincts because of my belief in the hard work ethic or because I was afraid to be out of work, to miss the right 'opportunity'. It was easier to think – who knows where this may lead? Yet, every time I ignored my instincts I paid the price down the line. And who knows what other opportunities I missed doing unsatisfactory projects. But I lacked faith, so I held on to my old beliefs. Don't make this mistake. Start cultivating faith now.

Even in my successful years on the West End I fell back into this fear mentality. I accepted an unpaid job in a gap I had between a paid tour and its West End run. I convinced myself that instead of resting I should squeeze another play in! I got the part in a fringe play and I should have been grateful for manifesting exactly what I had asked for. But I hated it.

I was too tired from touring. I didn't like the way the play was written or being directed. I felt annoyed that I had to trek through the snow to cold rehearsal rooms that lacked basic tea making facilities, let alone a paycheck, and I was grumpy. I just couldn't shake off my bad attitude because I knew I had betrayed my own judgement.

Furthermore, my negative attitude was spoiling the experience for some newer actors who were really delighted at this opportunity to work and get some exposure.

I knew that I should have let that opportunity go to someone who really wanted it, instead of panicking that I had a gap in my work schedule and being so desperate to fill it. It was too late to go back on my commitment, but not too late to look back and realise that I had known beforehand that it wasn't for me. It reminded me to pay attention to that instinct and to trust it. Listen to your gut, and when this is unclear to you then refer back to your specific vision and measure any opportunity against it.

Let's face it this is a crazy, challenging and difficult career to be in. You have to love it! Really love what you do! Why then would you accept projects your gut tells you that you won't love, that you'll hate or resent? Most of us are not in this for the money we're doing it because we love the creativity. If the project doesn't make your heart sing then it's not the project for you.

If you accept a job you know you won't love then you'll take the job away from someone who might love that role, the one you are doing to fill time, to avoid being 'out or work', to avoid *feeling the fear*. Don't avoid feeling the *out of work fear* because it is exactly that uncomfortable feeling that can propel you towards the objective you've set your heart on.

You must learn to say No. Not in a spoilt, entitled way, but in a focused, clear way. You say No because then you have the space to say Yes to what you do want. You are creating your path instead of just reacting to things being thrown at you. In fact, by saying No, you state what it is you do want as well. The No helps us get clear on the Yes. You say No because you believe this isn't the right opportunity right now, and you trust that the right opportunity will come.

One Christmas, I had been pushing and fighting and saying Yes to everything when I became ill. I knew I was ill from overworking and over committing. I needed to do less. I realised I needed a way to move my career forward, earn money and not burn out in the process. The universe provided me with such an opportunity by giving me a job understudying on a Number One tour.[5]

This was great because it got me away from my day jobs (yes plural) and the day I did working at my cooperative agency. In fact, as it was a tour, I got away from everything. I took a stack of books with me, several series of *Lost* to watch on my laptop (that'll date this story!) and spent mornings in coffee shops browsing the papers.

It was just what I needed until about week four, when I was rested and fired up anew, but was stuck on tour. I was not really in the family of the cast, definitely not in the show, and without my friends or even my home office to take forward any acting ideas I had, I started to feel completely isolated and introspective.

I said to myself, "never again". I told my agency on the phone, I wouldn't understudy on tour again. In fact, I wouldn't understudy unless it was on the West End. That was my new No and it defined my Yes. I will understudy but only on the West End. That way I could be in my home-town, sleep in my own bed and hang out with my friends and family. All of which helps to feed our emotional resilience.

Just like a wish, the next role I took was a role understudying on the West End, covering the lead in Jim Cartwright's *Little Voice*. I knew it was a fantastic opportunity, but I did not know at the time that I would make my West End debut. I was just ecstatic to have work, work that I wanted, that I had asked for. I felt in control of my career path. I felt I was advancing, even if I was still understudying.

And then, I got to go on. If you don't know the play or the film, the main character, Mari Hoff, is the most amazing female part: gritty, poetic and huge! I played eight shows in the lead actress' absence, gaining recognition from the Tony award winning director, the producer and owner of several West End Theatres, and the writer. Now I had been an understudy on the West End I needed to readjust my compass, to choose my next objective.

---

[5] An understudy in England is like being a cover in America. Although my understanding is that covers are respected in America for their ability to learn and play multiple roles where as in England the culture is different. Understudies are seen as lower down the pecking order. Perhaps because the word itself suggests both below the other actors (under-) and not quite ready (-study). This is a shame, because understudies have a difficult (albeit rewarding) job.

I told my agent I wouldn't understudy again, unless it was at the National Theatre. Another No. Another Yes. Three months after making this intention clear to my agent, and myself, I got an understudy job at the National Theatre in *After the Dance*, a Terence Rattigan play.

That's not because I had an amazing agent, I was represented by a wonderful cooperative agency, but theses agencies are less influential than personal management agencies. Nor was it because I was lucky. I did things to make it happen, some of which I'll look at later on, because they fall into other chapters, but the key thing here was that I got clear about what I would and wouldn't do.

I got very clear about what I wanted and decided that I would only understudy at the National Theatre. This made it clear for my agent and also I believe - when I wrote to the National Theatre - it made it clear for them. When you are clear people understand you better. Attention goes to the thing or person most easily understood. Where a confused mind says No, a clear view helps people say Yes. Yes to you. My passion to understudy at The National was 100% genuine, authentic and in alignment with my values and goals.

Understudying at the National Theatre meant getting to experience the thrill of going into London's most respected theatres. I worked at the National Studio on new scripts. I got vocal warm-up and training from the top vocal coaches. I got to experience going onto the National stage, being in the National Theatre dressing rooms, and walking the corridors where pictures hang of Dame Judi Dench and Sir Kenneth Branagh.

I had an inspiring time in a play that went on to win four Olivier Awards! I got to perform on the Lyttleton stage every night in the ensemble, and then in the role I had been covering for two extra shows, which were added on to meet the demand after the show sold out. I won't lie it was a dream come true.

I started to see the power of knowing what my next vision was and stating it clearly. I created a new No. I wouldn't understudy again unless there was a part for me. I didn't want to get stuck just understudying. I had proved I was reliable. I could learn multiple parts. But I wasn't a box office draw, because I wasn't known. I was more useful to producers as an understudy. Getting stuck at that level was a genuine concern. I needed to be seen by other industry influencers. Understudying did not guarantee that because either I might not get to go on stage at all, or I might go on too last minute to invite casting directors along.

Little Voice made me realise that some people are essentially professional understudies. I have huge amounts of respect for them. One actor I met understudied each male part in *Art*, which if you don't know the play is a three-man play. So basically he learnt the whole play by heart.

Understudies go on stage under higher pressure, to not let down the cast, producers or audience, yet they are usually under-rehearsed, under-paid and under-valued.[6] I didn't want to be a professional understudy. It's really hard when you are an actor watching someone else make the choices for the character that you have also learnt and thought about. It's tough, sitting back, watching them play the part. I wanted to act not sit on the equivalent of the subs bench.

But I still hadn't had to say No, not to a direct offer. I had said No in theory (No to understudying on tours, No to understudying unless it was at The National). I had told my agent not to put me forward for that work, but I hadn't had to turn anything real down. I had made my conditions but they had not been tested.

Then they were tested big time and with a huge, unforeseen affect.

I had just got out a loan, to pay for a new kitchen for my flat (part of my *Say No to rats in your kitchen strategy* – a whole other story). The point being, I was particularly vulnerable to fears about income and money at this time. I could have used this to justify changing my No. I was working at the National Theatre, in the show mentioned above. The end of the contract, and with it unemployment, was looming. The casting director of *Little Voice* called my agent and asked if I would audition to be the understudy in *Deathtrap*. It was a West End show starring the brilliant actor Simon Russell Beale. I was tempted.

But it went against my No – no more understudying unless there was a part. Logic argued that *it was only three months*, logic said *it was money for my kitchen*, logic said *it was a possible opportunity*, logic said *it was a compliment that ought to be returned by auditioning*. Insecure voices in my head said *who are you to say no? You aren't a big profile actor who can pick and choose. You haven't got that kind of weight behind you. Who are you to ask for more?*

But my gut said, No! I wouldn't be seen as an actor in my own right if I kept accepting understudy roles. I would get stuck as a professional understudy and I had paid my understudy dues. I looked at the script and also felt (in my gut) uninspired by the project. I knew it went against everything I had decided.

---

[6] Both in payment terms as – in my opinion - the Equity deal is not good, and by the audience who wants to see the star they came to see. One night, when they announced I would be playing the part of Mari Hoff, the audience groaned. It wasn't personal. They didn't know who I was. They were just disappointed and didn't know what they'd be getting (nor that I was on stage, behind the curtain in ear shot). Many understudies, replacing big names, have this reaction to deal with as well as their own nerves and the responsibility to both cast and producers.

So, I said No. I had stated that I wouldn't understudy again unless there was a part for me. I held my nerve and said No. My agent went back to the casting director and explained I didn't want to understudy any more. What did the casting director say? She said, "Good for her!" Which is a bonus in itself, but the story doesn't end there.

At a dinner for the cast and crew of *After the Dance*, the director asked me if I had a job lined up when the show finished. "Not yet," I replied. "Good, I'll speak to you after," she said. My heart froze. Speak to me about what? I could barely eat my food. What did she want? I was excited, hopeful, though of course the voice in my head jumped in with a story about how the director knew my *real* level and she was going to offer me some awful profit share job that I'd have to refuse.

We were a cast of about 20 with some really big names involved. If the director was approaching the understudy asking what she was doing next, I couldn't possibly believe it was to offer anything other than something really lowly. Again the voice of inadequacy yelled loudest. I'm sure you have heard those voices too. I tried to fight them, to be open to something amazing.

When the director and I finally sat away from the others she told me what she wanted and it wasn't a fringe show at all. In fact, she was putting on *Blithe Spirit* in the West End with one of my acting heroines Alison Steadman. The director hoped that actress Ruthie Henshall would play Elvira, but knew – even then - that Ruthie's other commitments meant she couldn't do all the shows in the tour.

She said she wanted me to understudy Ruthie, but she had spoken with her casting director and had heard that I wouldn't understudy anymore. It just so happened that the casting director she was using was the one who had asked me to audition for *Deathtrap*. My No to *Deathtrap* had led to this very conversation.

This was my real test, my chance to stick to my guns and say No, or rather to say Yes, she had heard right, I was not going to understudy anymore. I told her that I had worked my way up from the fringe for years, a decade in fact, and now I needed a part. It didn't need to be a big part. Even having a few lines being a maid would ensure I was on stage every night, and could get the exposure that I needed to further my career. She nodded. "Ok," she said, "Well the maid is a little young for you, but there might be this other part: the part of Mrs Bradman. She is normally cast older but I don't see that she has to be." The conversation ended with her saying she'd be in touch.

I couldn't believe it. I still have no idea how I managed to stick to my No in a conversation with one of London's most up and coming theatre directors and whilst she was offering me the chance to work with one of my heroines and to definitely go on in my understudy role. Here was me having the audacity to say, "Well, only on the condition that you give me a part *(as well)*".

I was being heard and respected, but more importantly my request was being considered. I believe the courage came from making the decision beforehand, before the decision ever got tested and from a new found belief in what I was worth. But be prepared, the braver and bolder you get, the bigger and louder the fear voice will speak up.

"Well, that won't happen!" said the inner voice, sticking to the story of my past experience, trying to protect me from getting my hopes up. But even though I clearly hadn't totally banished these limiting beliefs that I was not connected enough or good enough, I was acting and behaving from a totally different belief system. The voices were there but I heard them for what they were just voices. I was acting from a place where I deserved to move on from just understudying.

Three weeks later, three weeks of hoping and saying nothing to anyone (I didn't want to jinx it) my agent called me to say that they had offered me a part in exchange for taking on the understudying responsibilities as well. I could not believe my ears. I was in total shock. How had I gone from being a failed nobody to an actress who would be working on a West End show with the likes of Alison Steadman, with my own part and without even having to audition?

But though I asked the question in disbelief, I also knew exactly how it had happened. I had said No. I don't say all this to brag, but it was just one of the biggest lessons I've ever learnt and I hope that as well as sharing in my many failures you can learn from my successes too. There are lessons in both. I tell you because it shows that saying No gets results.

It's frightening, granted, but it is that courage that will be rewarded. As it was I had my dream realised. Every day I walked to Shaftesbury Avenue to the Apollo Theatre. Outside the theatre foyer was a large poster photograph of me, and my name was listed on the cast list with the principal cast. I was so proud. I had to work extra hard rehearsing with both the understudy cast and the main cast to be in both. But it was worth it!

Summary of lessons learnt

- Saying No brings clarity
- Clarity helps goal achievement
- Saying No means you have more time, energy and motivation to achieve your Yes work
- Having a list of criteria helps you assess each opportunity accurately to make important career decisions
- If you're gut says No, listen to that. Don't listen to the voices of fear
- As Dallas says, if it's not Hell Yeah, it's Hell No!

Strategy Four – Empower your words

We have all heard the expression *talk is cheap*. Anyone can talk. Few take action. Words about action - which are not followed up with action - are meaningless. It's easy to promise, to say you will do things you have no intention of really doing. Or have only half an intention of doing. Maybe you hope to do it, but don't have the discipline to follow up. Life gets in the way. Inertia sets in. Doing it involves a short-term cost, a sacrifice or an effort.

It might seem insignificant, natural even, to not follow through on what you say. Many people are what we might call *flaky*. It may seem that no real harm is done by flakiness. But I disagree. The harm is this: every time you do not follow up on what you said you would do, to others and even yourself, you disempower your word, and this has an impact far greater than you can imagine.

I grew up with parents who believed in an old-fashioned sense of honour: of taking pride in being a person of their word. It involves being honest with yourself and others. There are times when you cannot keep your word. None of us is perfect. But when you consistently and frequently say you'll do things you don't do, you weaken your personal power and your ability to create success in your life. If you say things but don't do them, you cease to become credible.

In this chapter we are going to seize back the power of our words. We're going to act on everything we say until our words become synonymous with action. What this means is that you become credible. It means you act on your words so often that people believe you when you speak. More importantly *you* believe you. Your body and your mind believe your words and on hearing them they prepare to act. They move towards that promise by seeking out opportunities, ideas and engaging the appropriate behaviours, all without you really trying.

Make words mean action

The interesting thing about being a person of your word is that the habit becomes automatic. It gets easier and easier to walk your talk because you will strengthen your word so much, that the mere fact of saying something now triggers your mind into a gear where it seems almost unstoppable. You have no choice now but to do what you've said, because that is what you've always done.

Your brain knows that words mean action. So even if you are afraid, if you can verbalise the action it's like burning a bridge, there's no going back. Before you know it, you too are performing stand-up, running a marathon, or publishing a book.

It's easy to think the words we say are not important. They are just words. But anyone who has studied linguistics or rhetoric, will tell you that words have power. Look at the power of words to persuade and inspire from Churchill to Martin Luther King. Or those used to mobilise people to commit heinous crimes. Think of the power of the media to influence its readers through the choice of words: whether they describe someone as a freedom fighter or terrorist.

If words did not have power, advertising companies would not spend millions coming up with slogans and taglines. They know that how they describe their product will influence our thoughts.

How we talk and describe ourselves, influences our thoughts. We think in pictures but we use words to pull up those pictures. Whether we think of ourselves as 'an actor' or 'a dreamer' is hugely relevant because it impacts how we feel and how we behave. How we act or do not act, whether we try or don't try, whether we believe or don't believe, all directly impact our success or failure.

Promises, commitments and statements of intent

Think carefully about those daily promises you make to yourself and others. I don't care how trivial they may appear. Think of those outer and inner statements such as, "I'll go to the gym today", "I'll drop an email to you later" and "I'd love to have you over for dinner" - how many do you actually follow up on and do? Not the ones where you actually use the words *I promise*, but everything else.

You might not think it is a promise, but if you say to yourself, *I'm going to go to the gym this week,* and you don't, somewhere inside you will feel upset by this broken promise. Even if you didn't tell anyone but yourself.

If you can't be honest with and keep promises with yourself, then it sends a deep message to you, from you, that you're not really trustworthy. Sometimes the message is just that you are not worthy. Not worthy of keeping a promise to. If you were meeting a friend at the gym, you'd show them the respect of showing up. So why would you give yourself less than that? Think about how that action, or inaction, impacts your self-belief and your self-worth.

Our beliefs are conclusions we have made based on information and/or experience. By repeatedly choosing to not follow through, you are building an experience of you. This negatively instructs the unconscious mind to ignore your words. Imagine if you promised me you'd be on time and you were late. I would forgive you. If you repeated this, I might be less forgiving. Over time, I would not only disbelieve you, when you said you'd be on time, but I would ignore you. I would have learnt from experience that you were not a reliable or punctual person. Your unconscious mind learns the same way.

When I am not true to my word, it hurts me somewhere; a tinge of self-disappointment, or something like that. It's hard to describe. I remind myself of this and it motivates me to choose the satisfaction of being a reliable person, a person of action, over that smaller lesser feeling. Even when it means doing something that is uncomfortable or scary in the short term, or it involves doing something that I simply don't feel like doing. Being alive means doing things we might be afraid of. Being disciplined means doing things we might not want to do (go to the gym, tidy the house), because we want the result of doing them (being fit, healthy and living in a clean house).

When I had thrown my hat into the ring to run a marathon I had never really jogged before. When we had done cross-country at school, I was usually last; I hated it. I had no understanding of long distance running or of pacing myself. I assumed I just couldn't do it or that I was too unfit. Now, aged 34, I had committed to my partner and a charity, to run 26.2 miles! I would wake up on running days wanting to stay in bed (I'm human after all!). But I knew the pain of not being true to my word would hurt more than the early start and the initial resistance to running.

I love my sleep and it is all too easy to stay in bed, especially on those dark, sometimes snowy winter mornings. It is far too easy to be motivated the night before and then resistant in the morning. Acting on your word is a choice that takes discipline, but like most actions, choose it often enough and it becomes a habit; the hard work will pay off.

How strong is your word? How well have you kept it so far? The test is this: ask yourself how your friends would react to you saying that you were going to climb Snowdon or take part in a charity run. Would they say, "Awesome, when?" or would they say, "Yeah, right" sarcastically? This will give you an indication of how true to your word you already are. If you do a lot of talk and don't follow through, people will doubt you and you will doubt yourself. This is fatal for an actor where self-belief can be the difference between booking a role and not, success or failure. But you can change this.

One way to change this bad habit is simply to start doing what you say you will. The second is to commit to fewer things, those you know you can and will do. Only promise what you can commit to doing 100%. Then ensure you do at least 98% of everything you say you will do from attending people's birthday parties to meeting deadlines, to eating healthier.

If you aren't going to do it, or if you are unsure whether or not you will, DO NOT SAY YOU WILL. Simple. Some people feel obliged to say things to be polite or to avoid awkwardness. "We must meet up" they say, when no one has any intention of doing so. Be braver than that.

If, like me you are an avid *Friends* fan, you will remember an episode where Chandler always tells his dates that he'll call them, even though he has no intention of doing so. He cannot deal with the uncomfortableness of their expectation, so he gives in and says what he thinks the women want to hear. Don't do that, it's weak. Get the power of your word so strong that when you say, *"I am going to be a successful actor"*. No one doubts it. Not even for a second. Then see how this impacts both your behaviour, how others treat you and your results.

Negative self-talk and silencing the Head Critic

Another form of words that can impact our ability to succeed is negative self-talk. These are the automated phrases that you repeat in your head on a regular basis, often without even noticing. Negative self-talk can come from your Head Critic who, like Statler and Waldorf (the Muppets in the theatre box), criticises everything you do, or simply mocks your attempts.

The Head Critic can appear on stage, pulling you out of being in the moment, with its negative observations on your performance. The Head Critic can be repeating negative phrases acquired in childhood from a teacher or parent. Such as the critic who thinks you are never good enough.[7]

Note your self-talk. Spend a few days listening to what you are saying to yourself. Are you calling yourself stupid, or lazy, or untalented? Are you repeatedly knocking your dreams and aspirations in ways you would never do to a friend? Our unconscious mind is always listening to our self-talk, positive or negative, and the most repeated patterns get reaffirmed and more wired in every time you repeat them. So, first, be aware of what they are. Start listening with your conscious mind. Write down the negative self-talk, or the words of the Head Critic. Expose them.

Self-talk can reveal limiting beliefs, we will cover these more in *Strategy Six*. But first, let's deal with Head Critic.

When I auditioned for the role of Lady Macbeth, I really wanted the role. I was hugely passionate about Shakespeare and Lady Macbeth is probably one of the most exciting female roles to play. Who knew when that opportunity might arrive again in my life, if ever? Furthermore, this production was going up to the Edinburgh Festival and playing at the Gilded Balloon, which was a great venue.[8]

---

[7] It might not be that we heard that exact phrase, but that we interpreted the other comments or reactions from adults to mean we were not good enough.

[8] Sadly, it burnt down later that year.

Everyone works for free on the fringe, in the hope of exposure, perhaps some profit-share, and the experience. As there is no budget, there aren't budget restrictions when it comes to people's time. Unlike those casting TV, for example, fringe productions can spend longer auditioning and can afford to see more people. So, whereas only four people will be called for a TV role, say, there were 100 women seen for the role of Lady Macbeth. The directors recalled three women. I was one of them. I was very excited. I went in and did my best. Then I just had to wait.

I don't know about you but I hate the waiting part. It feels powerless. Voices in your head try to protect you by imagining you won't get it. This is somehow supposed to save you the real disappointment of not getting it. I heard these voices, but decided to do something different. I really wanted the job, so I wasn't going to have this victim side win with its story of self-pity and failure.

I tried something new. Instead of not getting my hopes up, I got them up. I wrote down every reason why they should cast me in the role from my acting ability to my appearance to my attitude as a company member. Every time voices of self-doubt made themselves heard, I took out my piece of paper and re-read the list. I planned not for failure, but for success, until I didn't just hope for it, I expected it. I had made a very compelling list. I cancelled every negative thought with a positive one. Something I had never done before.

It seemed arrogant or risky to indulge in thinking I'd get it. Surely that was setting myself up for a fall. On the contrary, I set myself up for success. I got the part! At the time, I thought that maybe thoughts travelled in waves frequencies like mobile phone signals or radio waves. I imagined that while the director and producers were deciding who to hire, my positive messages came through. Perhaps it was the Law of Attraction at work.[9] I expected to get the part, and now the part was mine. But either way, I suggest you do this – if only to attack those ever-persistent limiting beliefs and negative self talk.

Bizarrely, the Head Critic is just trying to protect you. But the one thing I've learned for certain from life is that you cannot protect yourself from pain. If you can it is at the expense of experiencing all the joys of life. It's a choice really: you can accept the highs and lows or say No to both. But levelling out the highs and lows has always seemed like a flat line to me, and flat lining is what your heart does when it's no longer beating. To be alive, to really experience being alive involves risk. There will be some pain, chances to grow, but there will also be rewards for your courage, in love, in life, and in the achievement of your dreams.

---

[9] Discussed fully in *Strategy Six – Imagine*

It turned out getting the role of Lady Macbeth was not the end of my journey into either the Head Critic, nor the power of words. When I went up to Edinburgh to play the role, I suddenly realised I would get reviewed. Reviewers have a word limit so smaller roles (like those I'd been playing) are often not critiqued. But who was going to write a review on *Macbeth* and not critique the role of Lady Macbeth? No one.

I was worried. *What if they knocked me down?* Yep, straight into doubting and negative thoughts. *How would I recover?* I wondered. The reality is the more risks you take the more doubts you uncover. But at least now I had some new tools. So, back to the power of the pen. I decided to write my own reviews.

I wrote down what I hoped the critics might say. There are many actors who don't read reviews and think it's egotistical to concern yourself with reviews, but interestingly this exercise clarified for me, once again, my intent. And we've talked about the power of that earlier. I wrote down my intention to perform with believability. It worked. I got really good reviews. Now, I am not asking you to believe that my writing magically went into the heads of critics (though we can't be certain!) but I wanted to give you an example of the power of declaring in words, what you want to happen. It gave me back a sense of control and therefore confidence, whilst clarifying objectives in my mind.

The Head Critic may never go away, but once exposed we can make a better choice. We can hear the judgement and then put the Head Critic in its place, by saying, "Thanks for your feedback, but sshh now – grown ups are talking". Or simply say, "Delete." Once exposed you can re-write the negative phrases into positive ones. You rephrase and reframe them. Then use this as a new script to learn. Which as an actor shouldn't be hard to do. These positive phrases and new scripts are often called mantras and affirmations.

Mantras and affirmations

Affirmations are positive, present tense sentences which - when repeated often enough - can change belief patterns. If our thoughts stay the same we will make the same choices and act in the same way. This cements in the same old habits. In order to change these habits, we start with changing the words in our heads. Affirmations can be described as new thoughts; thoughts we choose to put into our unconscious.

The formula: Observe the negative thoughts and words you want to change. Write them down and then write down their positive equivalents in the present tense. Finally, repeat these daily, either by writing out the affirmations or saying them out loud. Speaker, author and coach, Bob Proctor, says these affirmations need to be said a thousand times a day, for 90 days. I believe he recorded his instead, so he could get maximum effect. Others try to speed the process up by talking directly to the unconscious mind via meditation, hypnosis and imagery. Some of which we will explore in *Strategy Six*.

A powerful way to turbo-charge your affirmations is to repeat them just before you go to bed. It is believed that whilst we sleep, our unconscious brain replays those thoughts (from the last 15 minutes before we feel asleep) the most.

As we drift off to sleep we are moving through various brain wave patterns as we slow down from Beta (awake) to Delta (deep sleep) via Alpha (relaxed but not asleep) and Theta.[10] Alpha is considered the 'gateway to the unconscious' because the unconscious is more easily influenced when it is in Alpha. This is why hypnosis and meditation are powerful states for change, and why we learn more effectively when we are relaxed.

Coach and author, Wayne Dyer, talks about the power of the five minutes just before you fall asleep – for this exact same reason. He says that most people spend this time reliving the mistakes of the day, when instead we should be planting positive thoughts into the unconscious mind whilst it is in Alpha. He suggests using the phrase *I am* followed by positive adjectives. e.g *I am content, I am grateful, I am blessed, I am healthy, I am strong, I am abundant* etc.

We will explore the unconscious mind further in the next chapter, but for the purpose of affirmations you need to understand this: the beliefs we need to change are in the unconscious mind, and the unconscious mind only understands the present tense. The unconscious mind is forever in the moment. This is why any communication with it must be made in the present tense. The unconscious mind will not understand an affirmation set in the future e.g *I will be successful*. Instead we must choose, *I am successful*.

There are some who say affirmations don't work unless you believe them. If that's what they believe, then that will be true for them. But others argue that the unconscious doesn't care if the conscious mind believes it or not. The unconscious, as we will explore in the next Strategy, is not discerning or analytical; it simply records and replays. Therefore, if it hears it enough, it will take it on as a fact.

---

[10] "…we all have five (Beta, Alpha, Theta, Delta and Gamma), and each frequency is measured in cycles per second (Hz) and has its own set of characteristics representing a specific level of brain activity and a unique state of consciousness."

Questions

Another helpful 'power of words' tool is questioning ourselves. The brain is like Google, and asking questions is like typing a topic into the search box. Our brain will find an answer so we need to be careful we don't ask questions such as: "Why am I always late?" or "Why can't I get this right?". If you want better answers they say, ask better questions.

Dallas recommends writing out some positive questions such as: "Why do all casting directors love me?" or "How did I suddenly get all these job offers?". Write them out on tiny strips of paper, fold them and place them in a bowl. Every day, reach in and pull out a positive question.

A wonderfully open question, which I read recently, was: *If I did know the answer, what might it be? If there were a solution, what might that look like?* This gives the brain scope to go through the massive database of our unconscious mind and find solutions. Compare this with closed comments; such as *I don't know how to do it*. This tells your brain, not to look, but to give up. You are instructing it, that you do not know. Life will improve when we use our brain to help us, not hinder us. Ask the right question then allow some time and space for answers to appear.

I am

The words we put after *I am* have impact also. Take care with your language about yourself. Note where you say something after *I am* that diminishes or disempowers you, and see if you can change it and make it positive. Then it becomes a powerful affirmation.

For me, one of the things I found really hard was saying that I was an actor. This is so often followed up with a question about what I have been in. If you have not been doing much, this can be a painful question. I often avoided saying I was an actor at all, which in some ways made it easier but had a negative impact on my own self-belief. Or I found myself diminishing the projects I was working on, "It's ***just*** a fringe show", "It's ***only*** a small part". What follows *I am* is powerful, so be careful (but also brave) about what you say next.

Mental diet

As we've covered so far, words have impact. This includes the words of others. Don't get involved in negative talk with others about your goals or the industry as again these inform our unconscious. We need to get stricter about our mental diet. Your mental diet is everything you hear, see, experience or read. The unconscious remembers it all, even when *you* are not paying attention. It has impact.

The unconscious absorbs what we watch and read, so the content of these informs our decisions, beliefs and behaviours. With that in mind, ask yourself this: *how positive is what you are reading or watching? What are the hidden messages that your unconscious will be picking up?* Watch powerful movies where people achieve their dreams. Swap gossip magazines, which are full of criticism and judgement for a powerful personal development book. These will improve your mental diet and you will start to cultivate a winner's mindset.

Don't be casual about who you hang around with (the words you hear). People may think they know about the industry, but they can't know it all. Even me. The industry is full of different people with different likes and dislikes so there will not be a perfect 'one-size fits all' strategy. Beware the advice you take as Gospel and the toxic talk you allow into your head, and consequently into your belief system.

Equally, your goals are your goals. You should talk about them, but you're not seeking approval. When someone reflects their fears onto you, you might have to brush it off, smile and move away.

You don't need to explain or justify yourself. The self-help industry calls them *naysayers*. They are afraid so they expect or want you to be. But your job is to be unafraid. Go and light the way. Don't battle with the naysayers they're not worth your energy. Sometimes a simple, but non-committal *you could be right* pacifies them, and you can move to a more positive and inspirational group whose words influence you for the better.

I wanted to end this chapter with the magic word, ***Abracadabra***. It means 'with my word I create' or 'with my word I influence.' It serves as a reminder that your words have power. You can use that power to propel your career.

Summary of lessons learnt

- Words are more than words, they are instructions to the brain

- Not being a person of your word, weakens your personal power

- If you say you will, then do it

- Negative self-talk blocks your path to success, so reframe negative thoughts

- Pay attention to the Head Critic but only to expose their lies and dismiss them

- Avoid hanging around with other critics, who talk negatively or toxically about their situations (and yours)

- Be aware of what your mental diet consists of and make any necessary changes

Strategy Five –Get over yourself

When I auditioned for *Little Voice*, I knew I had performed at my best. The casting director had said to me, "beautiful read" as she led me out of the room. But also I could just feel it in my bones. As actors, we know when we have been in flow, in the moment and all that other good stuff that makes for great acting. The next day my agent called to say that the director and casting director had loved me. I was on a heavy pencil awaiting final approval by the producers.[11] I was excited.

My first thoughts were positive. I knew I'd done well and this now confirmed it. But then, another voice piped up, the voice of the Head Critic. The critic said I would not get the part. That, although I had earned it and would be good at it, the decision was going to be made by people who hadn't seen me act - the producers. They would judge me on other things. I wasn't sure what the criteria might be, but I knew I would be found lacking.

This voice was familiar. It called itself *logic*. It called itself *experience*. But actually it was the voice of my *limiting beliefs*. Understand this is the voice of fear. The voice that thinks it is protecting you by not getting your hopes up, as we looked at in *Strategy Four*. But as we know, nothing can protect us from getting our hopes up. Our hopes are already up. These are our delicate passions and dreams.

We need to do two things. First we need to teach ourselves that we can cope with the disappointment of not getting the part, by making ourselves strong, happy, healthy, resilient and secure. Then, we go for a part and <u>decide</u> it can be ours.

By the time I was auditioning for *Little Voice*. I had already had the experience of both positively and negatively affecting my outcomes with my thinking. As you may recall, I used this technique when I was shortlisted for the role of Lady Macbeth. But the stakes were now really high – this was the West End! I took myself off to the ladies and had a talk with myself.

I listened a little while to my victim voice that said, "Yes, you're good enough for the role, but now the producers will be looking into you. The producers haven't seen your performance, so what will they be judging you on? Yes, judging you on your profile, which is low. Your risk level, which as an unknown actor, is high. That's why you won't get this."

---

[11] When an actor is reserved but not confirmed for the role, this is called 'a pencil', or 'to be penciled'. 'A heavy pencil' is still unconfirmed but is deemed more likely.

Another voice in me responded, told me to get it together. I heard the following words in my head: In order to get this, you have to believe it is possible. You have to believe it is possible for someone like you. You have to believe it is possible for you. I heard this second voice and decided to listen to it. I made an agreement with myself then and there to believe it could be me. I just decided it. A week later it was me.

We all have our story. The story of what our individual challenges and obstacles are. The story of why we haven't achieved our goals yet. It's because you're not lucky, you're too fat, you're too old, you just never get chosen, you're not good enough, and life is unfair. These seem like facts because we have some evidence for them but they are just beliefs.

These beliefs are called limiting beliefs, because all they do is limit you. Unlike the Head Critic, who sounds so obviously negative and critical, limiting beliefs disguise themselves as 'facts'. This makes them, in many ways, far more dangerous.

To understand how limiting beliefs are holding you back, often without you knowing it, we must take a detour into the workings of the mind. I am not a scientist so excuse the laymen explanation, but hopefully it will be enough to explain how the mind affects our behaviour and consequently our ability to achieve goals.

Roughly speaking, the mind is split into two sections: the unconscious (or subconscious mind) and the conscious mind. We often think the unconscious mind is where we dream from when we're asleep and the conscious mind is where we act from whilst we're awake. But in reality, the unconscious mind is affecting your actions and behaviours whilst you are awake and in a much bigger way than most people realise.

In fact, scientists believe that most of our decisions, actions, emotions and behaviour depend on the 95% of brain activity that is beyond our conscious awareness. This means that 95% of the time our unconscious mind, not our conscious one, is running the show. This means many of our actions and behaviours are on autopilot, invisible even to ourselves. We think we are in control, but unless we take back control, we are essentially running old programming.

All around us is data: light, colour, sound, objects, distance, people, verbal and audio information. The conscious mind cannot deal with much data in one go. So, it filters our environment choosing only the data it thinks we need to help us do whatever we're doing right now. This is why focus is so critical.

Our focus is a command to the brain to filter out anything outside of the scope of our focus. Imagine being in the dark with a head torch on. As you turn your head you illuminate the area within the light's beam. But you cannot see the other dark areas unless you turn your head (your attention) to them. And you can never illuminate the whole of the darkness with the head torch.

In the same way our conscious mind never has the complete picture. It only makes us aware of what we have asked our brain to look for —be that negative or positive. This is why witness statements vary so much from person to person; our filters, our focuses are all unique to us.

Our unconscious mind, however, has much larger processing capabilities, and so it can see the whole picture. Dr Lipton, author of *The Biology of Belief*, says that the unconscious mind operates at 40 million bits of data per second, whereas the conscious mind processes at only 40 bits per second. So the unconscious mind is a **million times more powerful** than the conscious mind.

From the womb until now your unconscious mind has taken in every image it has seen, every sound, every emotion. It remembers everything that has happened to you, even if you were physically unconscious (in an operation, for example). It doesn't filter. It is a sponge. It takes in everything, the good, the bad, and the ugly. This forms the basis of our programming, our conditioning.

With our conscious mind we may chose certain behaviours, for example, to be liberal minded. But our unconscious mind has taken in every stereotype and cultural myth, and unchecked, it is affected by those. The world's prejudices are all stored there, and affect our behaviour. This is called unconscious bias.

For example, in a chauvinistic culture women, as well as men, will have an unconscious bias against women because that is what their unconscious mind has absorbed from its environment. It is the unconscious mind that shapes our decisions and it is the quality of our decisions that shapes the quality of our lives.

What does this mean for you and your dreams of being an actor? Well, if your unconscious mind wants one thing, usually to keep you safe, and your conscious mind has a bigger, riskier dream in mind – then your unconscious mind will find ways to block you. This means you fail to achieve your goal, because as one part of you pulls one way, another part is pulling another way. You will be in conflict.

It is often hard for determined people to imagine they are in conflict. We feel committed. Our conscious mind is. But it is simply not as powerful as our unconscious mind. Trust me, if you can't achieve a goal you want, that is achievable by you, then you are in conflict. You might want success and fear it at the same time. Success comes with change and because change takes us into the unknown, it can be scary.

Let's look at weight, because it an easy parallel. Lots of people want to lose weight; many admit on a practical level that they're in control of what they eat. But somewhere in them they also want to stay as they are. It's safe and familiar. Becoming slim might bring unwanted attention. Becoming slim might make friends jealous. If you and your family all share being overweight together being slim might feel like a betrayal to them.

The unconscious mind doesn't care how silly or illogical any of these reasons are. It simply follows its old programming. You might diet then binge, or yo-yo diet. These are all helpful in that they show you are in conflict.

The fame or visibility that being a successful actor may bring with it might make many of us all feel afraid. We might want the spotlight but fear the scrutiny, want the fans but fear the trolls. Visibility means we are vulnerable, exposed, and that can make many people feel afraid. In this way, the unconscious mind is one of the key saboteurs to your dreams, not the economic climate, or the industry or whatever other reasons and excuses you may have.

One way to become aware of any conflicting beliefs is through our self-talk, which we touched on in the power of words. When you hear yourself say *I haven't done this **because**....* in relation to your goals, or you hear the words *I would **but**....* Then listen to what follows. That is your limiting belief. This is one of the beliefs that you have which is getting in your way. *E.g. I would go to drama school but I don't have the money. I haven't written to that director yet because I need more credits on my* résumé.

In fact, any belief you have about why you aren't where you should be, needs to be challenged. As we discussed, beliefs are thoughts that seem like facts because they have been in your mind for so long and you will have acquired a lot of examples to back them up. But remember this, an intelligent person can find evidence to back up any belief they want.

Furthermore, a person with one belief system will only see the evidence that supports that belief. It's one of the flaws of the human brain. Evidence that contradicts the current belief slips passed unnoticed or is seen and disbelieved. The current idea of *fake news*, for example, gives people the perfect excuse to disbelieve and ignore anything that doesn't align with their current belief system.

As an exercise, write down a list of the reasons why you believe you cannot or have not yet achieved your goal.

Here were some of mine:

- I am not connected enough (to influential people)
- My résumé doesn't have enough screen credits on it
- My agent isn't powerful enough

These appear to be facts, but they are all limiting beliefs. They limited me because they held me back. Furthermore, whilst I believed them, there are strong arguments to say I made them true, like a self-fulfilling prophecy. It seems illogical, but we all do it. We act in a way that brings about the experience we expect. We might not be happy but we are unsurprised and get to look 'right'.

We have to ask ourselves, "Do we want to be happy? Or do we want to be right?". Become aware of your limiting beliefs by writing down your excuses (disguised as reasons) and by listening to the talk you make to yourself and others, using phrases like "because…" and "but…".

Another way to do this is to imagine your objective, see yourself achieving it in the time you stated in *Strategy Two*. Notice what you might have started saying to yourself. *It's not possible because…. That time scale is unrealistic…. why would anyone choose me for the soap opera when there are so many other more experienced actors around?*

These subconscious beliefs may be totally opposite to what your conscious mind believes. For example, I may believe I am worthy, that I deserve success, but when opportunity comes knocking I am suddenly filled with self-doubt, *why me, perhaps I can't do it?* What we have then is totally opposing beliefs in the same mind, one in the conscious (you chose it) one in the unconscious (you didn't choose it).

Before we can align our unconscious beliefs with our conscious mind's plan, we must banish the limiting beliefs, or at least rattle their 100% status. By 100% status, I mean that at the moment, you believe these beliefs to be facts. It is not a limiting belief, or an excuse to you; it is the reality of the situation. And I am sure you can back it up with examples.

Let's shake up a belief that seems to be factual.

One of my limiting beliefs was: There aren't enough roles for women, even less for older women.

I could back this up with evidence from unions (statistics and everything!) as well as watching television and seeing how few roles there are out there. In fact, I used to look at all the film posters on my commute into London and tally up the male/female role ratio: this film - five men one woman, that film - six men etc. I could sit with my friends and discuss it. They'll most likely agree or I'll persuade them, and then my belief gets firmer.

As far as I am concerned this is not an opinion it has become a fact. Then I have no faith and no chance, because who would take action towards an unachievable goal? Only an idiot right? That is how these beliefs hold you back.

If you are doing these things become aware that you are your own worst enemy. You are in your own way. Try to do them less and less. Instead challenge the belief and say, ok, maybe there aren't as many roles for women (yet), but I am only one person so, at any one time, I can only do one role, how many roles do there need to be?

Perhaps I start looking at all the evidence that more and more women are becoming writers, producers and directors. I could look at Sally Wainwright and the fantastic amount of roles she writes for women, women who aren't all young or skinny. I could see the tide as turning.

Let's knock another one down. Get brutal here; these thoughts are holding you back.

Next Limiting belief: I am not talented enough to get a television role. I don't have enough credits.

Ok, now I am going to look at it objectively (as if it is not about me, but a friend's belief) and ask: *Do you need to be a good actor to be on television?* Having seen bad actors on television as well as good ones, I say No. So even if I am not a good enough actor yet, that's not necessarily relevant. Talentless people still work on television.

Then there is my second point: *I don't have enough television credits.* Yes, people probably feel safer when you have some television credits down already. But logic tells us that everyone who has ever been on TV had to make their first appearance at some point - a point when they too had no TV credits.

If one person has done it then the belief is not a fact, it might be a probability but it is not a fact. And if it were not a fact why would you use it as a reason to stop putting yourself out there. Why would you give it your time and energy?

You may still send your emails, but if you believe that ultimately people will scan your résumé and decide you don't have enough credits, then that negative energy will be there in your letter. It will put people off taking the risk, which in turn will continue to justify your limiting belief. Whatever your limiting belief is, that is what will show up for you.

Now, you can do the above exercise in partners if you get stuck and feel convinced that your limiting belief is a fact. Which believe me, some of them will feel like. But it's better if you can use your own brain to challenge the beliefs yourself. This is because other people challenging you might make you defensive and hold onto your belief even harder. So if you do work with a partner, chose someone you trust and decide to be open.

Our brains are very clever search engines, as we know. Someone mentions a new place or a new word to us, and then suddenly, now it's in our sphere of knowledge, we see it everywhere and wonder how we didn't know of it before. This can happen with positive things and negative ones too. If we believe something negative we naturally seek for proof of this and find what we are looking for. Not because it is true, but because we are seeking it.

I take this list from Brian Kim's website at www.briankim.net, he says beliefs are hammered in, over time, and new beliefs need to be given the same treatment. He suggests we do the following:

- Write the new belief down or say the belief out loud daily – See affirmations in *Strategy Four*

- Put it up everywhere so you can see it – this helps the mind take it in

- Associate with those who share that belief – as they will help solidify it

- Look for proof that your belief is true – as you have been doing with your negative beliefs

- Make a record of this proof in a belief conformation journal – the power of writing it down, helps record it in the mind

- Take action. If we act from our new belief we will reinforce the words

- Acknowledge any progress – this is similar to recording the proof, but might also be where you observe the changes in yourself. You see yourself acting from a different place and therefore acting differently

As we discussed in *Strategy Four*, we are trying to communicate with the unconscious mind. It is worth understanding this part of your brain and how it works. This will make your efforts to change more effective. Will power alone can't compete with the power of the unconscious mind where these beliefs are held.

What we are doing here is forming new mental habits. This takes work and takes time. Be patient and don't give up because its taking time, anything worthwhile is worth waiting for and if you have your mind trained then you have the most valuable tool in the world.

You might feel as I have at times, as if you are being asked to ignore reality, to lie to yourself about how the world is or even as if you are being told to brainwash yourself. And partly you are right. We are attempting to brainwash ourselves except this time we are programming in positive beliefs instead of negative ones. We need what Tony Robbins describes as *certainty*, in order to succeed. When we are certain, he argues, we take massive action, see massive results and then become even more certain. But whilst we have doubts, we act from that place, and this negatively impacts our results.

As for ignoring reality, there is no one reality. We all see the world through the lenses of our experiences and no one has a clear view. So, if a clear view is impossible and we must wear lenses we might as well <u>choose</u> the lenses. Limiting beliefs were our old lenses, we didn't choose those, we were given them. They are negative lenses, which were meant to keep us safe, but now they just hold us back.

Life tends to deliver what we expect. Positive lenses won't guarantee an easy ride either, but the view will be better, more hopeful and you'll be a nicer, more inspiring person to be around. If you are going to create a self-fulfilling prophesy, let it be "I'm so lucky", not your old mantra of "Nothing good ever happens to me".

Summary of lessons learnt

- Trying not to get your hopes up is <u>not</u> a positive post-audition tactic

- Dismissing the negative voices <u>is</u> a positive post-audition tactic

- Understand that most of our actions, behaviours and habits are done unconsciously

- Our unconscious is filled with everything we've ever heard and seen – whether we wanted to remember it or not

- Our unconscious mind may <u>not</u> be aligned with, or agree with, the goals of our conscious mind, impacting our ability to succeed

- Limiting beliefs can be observed, challenged and turned into positive beliefs

Strategy Six – Imaginate

"You, through the power of your own thoughts, are the most influential person in your life. Which means there is nobody more effective at undermining your success – and nobody more effective at supporting your success." Jeff Olson, *The Slight Edge.*

We've looked at how our words and negative beliefs affect our success. Now, I want to explore the exciting theories that suggest we can create our reality with our thoughts. To me, Imaginate is to create with your imagination. If this is a new concept to you, it may sound a bit 'out there', but stick with me whilst we look at the evidence, both anecdotal and scientific. In *Strategy Two*, I argued for defining a goal that was 100% in your power to deliver. But for those who believe we create our own reality, then everything is 100% in our power to deliver. Surely we need to ask: *could we – as actors – use one of our strongest skill sets (imagination) to realise our dreams?*

The first time I came across anything akin to this concept was when I watched the film *The Secret. The Secret* explores a theory called the Law of Attraction, which claims that we can manifest our desires, using our thoughts.

The theory became mainstream when *The Secret* was released in 2006, though there are also plenty of other books on the subject. The thinking is that our thoughts and feelings have an energy and therefore an energetic frequency. This frequency, or vibration, will draw to it anything else that resonates on that same frequency.

Everything in the world is made up of energy and everything is vibrating even if this is not visible to the naked eye. High frequencies (positive or good feelings) attract other high frequencies to them (experienced as positive situations). Low frequencies (negative or bad feelings) attract low frequencies to them (experienced as negative situations).

In this way, our thoughts (frequencies) are attracting to us everything in our life. As we can choose our thoughts (unless we are unconscious and in our programming) then we can choose our frequency. If we don't like what we are attracting we can change our frequency, by changing our thoughts.

In *The Secret*, author Rhonda Byrne states, "Your current thoughts are creating your future life. What you think about the most or focus on the most will appear <u>as</u> your life... Thoughts are magnetic and have a frequency...you are like a human transmission tower, transmitting a frequency with your thoughts."

The theory has its fans and doubters, but whatever you believe, there is now mounting scientific evidence in both neuroscience and quantum theory that supports the idea that we create our experience of reality from the inside out. We will look at these further in this chapter.

The Law of Attraction

The three steps for the Law of Attraction are simplified to Ask, Believe, and Receive. But I think it's more helpful to think of the process as:

- Visualise what you want (focus and imagination)

- Feel the emotion that would accompany having your desire realised (raising your energy vibration)

- Trust and believe that the outcome will manifest (faith/surrender)

Here's what happened when I tried out the Law of Attraction to advance my acting career and fulfil a life-long dream. You may remember from earlier chapters that at 35, I had decided I wanted to understudy at the National. I had written to the National several times over the previous months, but also knew that they received hundreds of letters from actors. I had just seen *The Secret* and thought I would have nothing to lose by trying the Law of Attraction. It started out as a bit of harmless fun.

First, I changed my screen saver to a picture of the National, that way I had a visual that I saw daily (*vision and focus*). I also stuck a picture of the theatre in my gratitude journal.[12] This was a journal I had that listed everything I was grateful for. I added to it daily, though this was the first time I had included something that was not yet in my life. I wrote a powerful affirmation, saying how excited I was to be working at the National Theatre and what a wonderful summer I was having on the riverbanks of the Thames.[13]

The Law of Attraction states that **like attracts like**. So to attract the role at the National, I had to feel in that present moment, the energy of having that role manifested. That energy for me was: excitement and gratitude.

The next day my plan was to start walking to the National's stage door, to train my brain to expect that in the future. This is something called *Acting As If*. You act as if what you want has already materialised, raising not only your energetic vibration but also programming your brain to expect this as a future reality.

By involving the body too, I was taking my physical energy to the place of my focus. It was just an experiment. What did I have to lose? Yet, before I had time to rehearse going to the stage door, my agent called to say the National Theatre had asked me in for an audition the very next day.

It was surreal.

---

[12] We will discuss the gratitude journal in the final chapter, though it is as it sounds. Please note that these affirmations must be written in the present tense, as if you are experiencing the joys of having attained that desire now.

[13] Note this is in the present tense.

I auditioned the next day, had a recall the day after and by 4pm the third day I had the job. Just as I had written in my journal, I spent a wonderful summer on the Southbank in a play that went on to win four Olivier awards and sell out. I know it sounds incredible, but that is how it happened for me.

You might think that this sounds like a coincidence. But what if it is not? What if, as some argue, there are no coincidences? I had written to the National before and not received an audition. So, why now? Why did this unlikely audition come my way just as I had followed the rules of the Laws of Attraction and Vibration? I decided that it was worth exploring if we have more power than we think.

I then looked back at other successes (and the failures too) in my life. Sometimes we think our successes are flukes or random. But what if they are not? If we learn how we did it in the past we can recreate it. In *The Secret,* Byrne states that the Law is always working for us; bringing what we think about the most, be it negative or positive. Having learnt about the Law of Attraction from *The Secret* I realised I had been using some of the laws already to manifest the roles of Lady Macbeth (and the reviews) and Mari Hoff.

Thoughts are energy

There is plenty of evidence that thoughts are indeed magnetic and have a frequency. The medical profession already measures electrical signals in the brain with an EEG (electroencephalogram). They can also use an MEG (magnetoencephalogram) to map and record magnetic fields produced by those electrical currents. If you want to see how magnetic energy can influence matter, place a magnet above some iron filings and watch them defy gravity. The scientific facts are that our thoughts and emotions do have an energy, and energy can influence matter.

In his book, *You Were Born Rich,* Bob Proctor writes, "when you hold the image of your goal on the screen of your mind, in the present tense, you are vibrating in harmony (resonance) with every particle of energy necessary for the manifestation of your image on the physical plane. By holding that image, those particles of energy are moving toward you (attraction) and you are moving toward them – because that is the law."

Things are not as they seem

It might all sound a bit strange, but reality is not as it appears. Let's take sight. It feels as if we look out on a world that is 'out there'. That seems like common sense. In reality, the eye takes in light waves and the brain uses this to create a picture of the 'reality out there'. If you were given glasses that turned the world upside-down, your brain would quickly adjust the picture and turn the world around again. What this tells us is that our brain does not simply reflect the outside world. It creates ***its*** vision of reality.

Everything you and I experience through our senses, we experience essentially through the brain. The brain, as we discussed in the last chapter is <u>not</u> objective. It delivers what we want or expect, not necessarily what is there. When we open up to the idea that the world is not limited to what we experience, or by what appears to be 'common sense', then we open up a world of possibilities.

In many ways, we have accepted that what we see isn't the whole picture. We know, for example, that there are stars we can see that are no longer actually there. We accept that there could be bacteria on our kitchen surfaces that aren't visible to the naked eye. Yet, on the other hand, we still struggle with other scientific facts, because they haven't been absorbed by the mainstream culture and so they sound too 'weird'. But reality is not as it appears and if we dive into the quantum level, even the laws of physics come unstuck.

Quantum physics examines the behaviours of the smaller world of atoms and subatomic particles. It has been discovered that at this level matter no longer behaves as we would expect. That is to say that the laws of classical or Newtonian physics do not apply in the quantum world.

On a quantum level, matter, the objects we perceive as solid (book, table, chair, person) are not solid at all. In fact, they are 99.9999999999999% empty space. In his book, *Quantum Theory Cannot Hurt You*, Marcus Chown states that, "If there was some way to squeeze all the empty space out of the atoms in our bodies, humanity would indeed fit into the space occupied by a sugar cube."

That seems incredible. But it is a scientific fact. This means that just because something seems unbelievable, doesn't make it untrue. And yet, we haven't got to the exciting bit yet: the part that connects this science to our power to manifest. Quantum physics has revealed that this space is not empty. It just *appears* to be.

"The quantum vacuum is actually a seething morass of microscopic particles such as electrons popping into existence and vanishing again...the laws of nature that usually prevent things from appearing out of nothing appear to turn a blind eye to events that happen too quickly", writes Marcus Chown. If an electron can appear out of nowhere, could our visions also manifest from that same nowhere?

Furthermore, experiments show that an atom can behave like a particle or a wave.[14] Whether it is particle or wave, solid or not solid, depends on whether there is an observer watching the particle. What might this mean to us? Well, observing is the focus part of the Law of Attraction. Could the act of observing what we want change the atom from wave form (not yet materialised) to particle form (materialised)?

Quantum physics gets even weirder, but no less scientific! An atom (until observed) can be (or has the potential to be) in all places at once. It exists everywhere until we focus on it, then it materialises.

In the quantum field all possibilities exist, we just need to select (observe) the one we want. As Jim Al-Khalil explains in his book, *Quantum – a guide for the perplexed*, "the quantum world may seem unbelievable to us when judged according to the prejudiced views of everyday experiences – what we call common sense. But the alien way that quantum objects behave is beyond doubt. A single atom can travel down both roads....they can sample all possible experiences simultaneously."

To review: matter is not solid, it just appears to be. How matter behaves, depends on us observing it. Atoms can be in all places at once and electrons can appear out of nowhere. With those factors in mind, using energy (our thoughts) to influence matter (our desires) seems less insane.

As Dr Joe Dispenza, author and neuroscientist, writes in his book, *You Are the Placebo*: "if you can imagine a future event that you want to experience in your life, that reality already exists as a possibility in the quantum field – beyond this space and time – just waiting for you to observe it. If your mind (through your thoughts and feelings) can affect when and where an electron appears out of nowhere, then theoretically you should be able to influence the appearance of any number of possibilities that you can imagine."

Visualisation

One of the things that can block the manifestation of our desires is – surprise, surprise – the unconscious mind. As you may remember from the previous chapter, our minds can be in conflict. You might want to manifest something, using the Law of Attraction, but unconscious beliefs that it won't work or that it's unsafe for you to have the desired result will block you.

For every powerful positive thought, you may have 20 negative *this won't happen* thoughts. We have discussed how to use words to reverse these odds and reprogramme the unconscious in the previous two chapters. Now we are going to look at the power of imagery and the imagination.

---

[14] Double slit experiment, for example.

Visualisation is a tool that uses our imaginations to programme success into the mind. Sometimes called *mental rehearsal*, visualisation is a physical experience whereby you imagine the entire experience you want to create. It should involve as much detail and emotion as possible.

From a chemical or feeling perspective, the brain cannot distinguish between a real and an imagined event. If you imagine a stressful event, or have a distressing dream, the body experiences it as if it were real. Dr Joe Dispenza suggests that practising in the mind creates an experience for the brain to learn from. Giving it a map, if you will, for that future event.

I attended a workshop once for commercial castings and the teacher said he asked the most successful advert actor what his secret was. The actor had said he read the script visualising himself playing the part, went into the room with the energy as if it were already his, and then on the way home he imagined himself on set, having the job. He was using visualisation. He expected to get the job. He imagined himself there and how good he'd feel. He acted *as if*. As a consequence, he was successful. I am sure there were times when he didn't get the job, but he has raised the odds in the areas over which one might argue he has no control.

Visualisation is a way we can use our thoughts to practise in perfection (before an audition) or dress rehearse disaster. Clearly we want to do the former and cease imagining the worst. Visualisation is now a common and powerful tool used by many people to enhance performance, from Olympians to business professionals to actors. With practice, visualisation can become so real that athletes imagining performing actually increase muscle strength (without lifting weights), raise their heart rate (though they are stationary), and can even break out into a sweat.

Actor, Jim Carrey, is a massive advocate of both visualisation and the Law of Attraction and told Oprah, "I would imagine having film directors interested in me, saying, *you know, I like your work*".[15] He is famous for writing himself a cheque for $10m, years before he got paid the exact same amount for starring in the film, *Dumb and Dumber*.

Vision Boards

Another powerful tool is a vision board. This is a visual representation of everything you want to attract into your life. As you pin pictures to the board you are metaphorically pinning the pictures into your unconscious so that your brain can seek out ways to achieve and attain them.

---

[15] http://www.oprahmag.co.za/live-your-best-life/career/jim-carrey-shares-his-success-secret-with-oprah

Your brain is seeking all the time, like the search facility on the Internet. The vision board puts things into the Google search of your brain, if you will, and then alerts you when it sees something helpful: a seminar run by the director of the show you want to be in or an instinct to see a certain show and then to follow up with the writer perhaps.

These ideas, generated by our own internal search engine must then be acted upon and followed up. Your first thought to do so should not be ignored. Act quickly before the self-doubt paralyses you.

Start collecting magazines and newspapers, then sit one evening with some music on (glass of wine optional) and pull out any pictures that resonate with you. These can then be pinned to a vision board in separate areas, health, fitness, home, relationships, career etc. In the centre of the board should be a picture of you, one you love, where you are happy. Simply looking at the board should raise your vibration, as you see and feel excited about your vision.

On the Internet there are also movie equivalents of vision boards such as *Mind Movies*. But if you are experienced enough, you can make your own movies with images, inspiring music and some affirmations of gratitude. Whatever most absorbs you in the visualisation process.

Be patient for the results too. We're planting and watering seeds but they might not bloom for a season, or a year. Just because they are under the earth and therefore invisible, does not mean the shoots aren't growing, or that your effort (energy) has been in vain.[16]

If you make this fun and playful, then it will never be in vain because you will have had fun. Having fun will make you more creative, more relaxed, and less likely to start controlling and pushing. Once you need that audition or that break, rather than playfully and passionately desiring it, then your energy will not attract it. In his book called the *Law of Attraction*, Michael Losier calls this surrendering process 'allowing'. Allowing is the absence of doubt, because doubt itself is a negative emotion that lowers your vibration.

Around the time of the BAFTAs (British Academy of Film and Television Awards), I posted a status update on my Facebook, which read, *I wonder why my BAFTA invite hasn't turned up yet?* I knew full well I wasn't on the list. I was not an A-lister. I hadn't done any big films or TV shows, and I wasn't a member of BAFTA. At that time, I had understudied on one West End show – that was it. The Facebook joke was light-heartedly mocking my own status as an unknown actress.

---

[16] It should not be an effort. See *Strategy One* –Give up the fight.

Then the day before the BAFTAs, the producer from the West End show I had just done called me out of the blue. She had been at a pre-BAFTA party and had sat next to an American film financer. He had just discovered that his tickets to the BAFTA awards (and the post award party) were for <u>two</u> and he didn't have a date.

The producer said she could find him a date, she knew loads of actresses, but he said he needed someone who wasn't just arm candy. He needed someone who could be left alone and cope, if he needed to talk business. She thought of me.

Of course, I said Yes! I did, however, have to borrow a dress, buy some costume jewellery from Claire's accessories and get my head around the fact that little me was going to the BAFTAs. I got picked up by the financer's chauffeur (like someone in a movie) and driven to his London hotel, then on to the ceremony.

We walked the red carpet and had VIP entrance to drinks before the show. Then afterwards we went to a big producer's party (are we allowed to discuss Harvey Weinstein anymore?) where award winners such as Carey Mulligan were there.

We cannot understand how the universe might bring us something, but a playful wish, and there it was. Unbelievable but true.

If you are hitting resistance over this, then ask yourself: what are you afraid of? Is this topic bringing fears to the surface? It might feel safer to be cynical. Whatever your resistance is about, be curious and find the opportunity to learn and grow. If we believe the Law of Attraction won't work, then it won't. We can feel happy that we're right. Equally, if we are desperate for the Law of Attraction to work, it won't, which reminds us not to push, but to be proactive, then patient.

I admit I have tried to manifest other goals with the Law of Attraction and not managed it. Perhaps I held some of those desires too tightly. Maybe some are still on their way. But there are too many people with similar stories to mine to dismiss the theory of the Law of Attraction entirely.

Thoughts can heal

Alongside, or perhaps separate to the Law of Attraction. Thoughts do have a significant influence over our lives. On a biological and chemical level our thoughts have been shown to have huge significance. What we think instructs our brain to produce a chemical (the feeling) and this has now been shown to impact our genes: activating or deactivating them.

Our genetic potential is not fixed, as we once believed; it just appears that way because we activate the same genes again and again, by thinking the same thoughts. Out of the 40,000–60,000 thoughts you have today, 90% will be the same thoughts you had yesterday. Psychologists estimate that 70–80% will be negative and redundant.[17] This means we are in *Groundhog Day*, creating the same reality and wearing out the same genes.

"Your beliefs act like filters on a camera, changing how you see the world. And your biology adapts to those beliefs. When we truly recognize that our beliefs are that powerful, we hold the key to freedom. While we cannot readily change the codes of our genetic blueprints, we can change our minds and, in the process, switch the blueprints used to express our genetic potential. " Bruce Lipton, *The Biology of Belief*.

Think new thoughts and you will create new feelings, which releases new chemistry into the blood sending a totally different instruction to your cells. This instruction activates a different set of genes and generates a different biological result. This is called epigenetics.[18]

In *You Are the Placebo*, Dr Joe Dispenza lists multiple case studies showing how people who were unknowingly taking a placebo (a sugar pill, or mock operation) healed themselves. They didn't just feel better in the mind; they were physically better in their bodies. They healed themselves by generating the required chemistry to match the sickness and this was done by belief (thought) alone. He writes, "As soon as you think a new thought you become changed – neurologically, chemically and genetically".

The Thought to personality connection

On a practical level, what we think impacts how we feel and consequently how we experience reality. Let's take two people, both get stuck in traffic on their way to work and then go to a meeting where they are made redundant. Person A thinks the traffic was annoying and the news devastating. Person A experiences a rubbish day.

Person B expects traffic, understands they too are part of the traffic, and doesn't let it affect their mood. They interpret the redundancy as a sign they should try something new and feel excited about how they are going to spend their redundancy cheque.

---

[17]   https://www.forbes.com/sites/davidkwilliams/2015/09/23/exceptional-leaders-create-an-awareness-of-greatness-in-the-workplace/#54f78407227f

[18] If you want to read more on this, I recommend *The Biology of Belief,* by Dr Bruce Lipton (or watch his many YouTube videos).

Person B has not experienced (from a feelings perspective) the same day as Person A. Yet, what happened to them in the outside world was the same. The difference was what they thought and felt about those experiences.

Whatever is going on for us we can always choose our thinking. We might have an automatic reflex that isn't positive. This is normal. Let it pass. Don't act on or continue this initial reaction. Pause. Then make a new choice. This will impact your entire experience of reality and also who you become.

Dr Joe Dispenza states that if a feeling is felt for a long time then it becomes a mood. If extended, this mood becomes a temperament. Extend the temperament and you have a personality trait, i.e. who we think we are. Who we are is only fixed by us choosing the same choices every day. We can change who we are by changing the thoughts, or at the very least – how long we have those thoughts for.

Cary Grant famously said, "I spent so long being Cary Grant, that I became Cary Grant." Meaning that if you think the thoughts of the person you want to be, you will feel like the person you want to be, you will act as the person you want to be, and you will, over time, become that person. But it has all just been patterns of thought. This is the power of thought.

Summary of lessons learnt:

- Like words, thoughts have power

- Thoughts have a measurable energetic charge

- The Law of Attraction states that you can change your life by changing your thoughts

- We are all made of energy and can change our frequencies up or down

- High vibrations (feeling good) attract high vibration experiences

- Thinking the same thoughts lead to taking the same actions and therefore delivering the same outcomes

- If you want a future different from your past, you need to change your thinking

- Thoughts impact our brain chemistry and consequently our health

- Visualisation and mental rehearsal are powerful tools for change

Strategy Seven - Know you, be you

"Be you, everyone else is taken." Oscar Wilde

When you play a well-known role such as Lady Macbeth, the many famous actors who have played the role before you can haunt you. You want to be true to the text and the character, but you don't want to be a carbon copy of those who have already played the role.

This plagued me when I played Lady Macbeth. How could I be unique and add something without changing the essence of the role? One of the co-directors wisely taught me, that my Lady Macbeth was already unique by the virtue that I was unique. I brought my own individuality to the role without trying, as any actor would, because none of us is identical.

However...whilst of course you are a unique and special human being, within the *business of show* you are also a brand, a product. Other people will perceive you as a type of product even if you are unhappy with the label. You might as well know what brand you are, so that you can use this to your advantage. Knowing who you are helps define your brand and makes marketing more effective. In this chapter we will look at how to find out what your brand is so you can use that to improve your marketing and increase your chances of securing auditions.

When I left drama school like many I didn't secure an agent. In fact, I didn't get a single interview. It can be a hugely stressful experience going to your graduation showcase, leaving out the required 20 CVs only to discover fellow students, or perhaps you, have counted and calculated who has been the most popular; who has been successful.

I can share with you now that I had only three out of twenty résumés taken. Low odds of getting agent. No one called me in for a meeting. Drama school was over and I didn't have an agent. I felt devastated. It was my first taste of industry rejection.

I felt it reflected on my ability as an actor. And whilst others and I felt we were not good enough, other people in more niche brackets were getting inundated with offers. They too, believed this reflected on their talent. When I later worked as an agent I discovered we were all wrong.

As drama students we may have been told how agencies operate here in England, but I think we all thought (or perhaps hoped) it would work as it does in the States. In America an agent will represent or take on anyone they think can get work and earn them a commission. If two or three actors within the same agency go up for the same part, the attitude is one of *let the best man win.*

In England, the agencies will try and take on the broadest spectrum of clients possible because they don't want clients competing against each other. This means the agent can focus on individual clients with more devotion and hopefully (for agent and client) get their client more work. The drawback is that it limits the amount of actors in the UK who can physically be represented. This provides a good filter to an over-subscribed industry but it is not a filter based on ability.

For example, in the agency I worked in we had several actresses who were mid-twenties, white and middle class. To ensure no one clashed with them we didn't interview other actresses who were in this casting bracket - even though their show reels and letters were usually better than those of other groups. Whether they were good actors or not didn't come into it. How hard they had worked, didn't come into it. We were actively seeking to fill less populated brands for more niche roles, be they Scottish, those with musical theatre skills, Asian, East European or larger sized actors.

It doesn't sound politically correct, but then the acting industry isn't. It can't be. If there is a role of a fat, sleazy man in a film, the writers, casting directors and directors need to be able to write a breakdown asking for a fat, sleazy man, and agents want to have one on their books to submit.

Popularity of brands can follow certain trends. There was a time when most English actors spoke Received Pronunciation (RP).[19] Then diversity was embraced and people with regional accents increased in visibility. Now, as chunks of the BBC move out of London (where RP dominates) into Bristol, Cardiff and Manchester, it is likely that we will hear fewer RP accents, and that more local actors with regional accents will be used. [20]

Art reflects life and vice versa, so sometimes it is politics and current affairs that dictate which niches will be popular. For example, the current influx of Eastern Europeans into Britain means an increase in roles for Eastern European speakers and actors who can do an Eastern European accent. Writers are writing these roles into modern scripts creating a new demand which casting directors and agents need to respond to.

These people are not better actors; they are just offering a different brand up to the market; a brand that's in demand. Simply as a consequence of current affairs then, some actors work more and succeed where equally good actors are stuck waitressing or doing TIE.[21]

---

[19] RP is the accent typically understood to be the standard British form. In period drama you will get RP or heightened RP, which was the accent, anyone of the upper classes would have spoken. RP accents dominated in the sixties because it was attached to class and education, so even those who did not have the accent, would quickly try and assimilate it.

[20] British Broadcasting Corporation, owner of four television channels and seven radio stations.

[21] Theatre in Education is the name for when plays are toured around schools for educational purposes, often with a workshop or Q&A between pupils and the cast

It can be disheartening. You can't change current affairs, or your brand. Well, I could become a man to open up more roles, but it would be extreme! So, what can you do? First you can get familiar with your brand. You may or may not know what it is and even if you do your brand will change as you age.

At 35, my brand was yummy mummy, or middle class authoritative figures (lawyers, senior doctors, psychiatrists), I played charismatic bitches (and didn't take it personally) and I had a quirky, comedy edge too, courtesy of an odd chin. If it sounds a bit like type casting then you would be right, that is exactly what it is.

I know, as actors we want to play a range of roles, to show our versatility, to act! But we have to get realistic about how the industry works, so we can use it to our advantage. How it works is that until, or unless, you are a big name (famous), then you will play your type, your most obvious brand. Only once you are powerful enough, i.e. your name is a huge draw, can you or will you be asked to play other types.

Some people make a fantastic living playing to type. Others play to type but then when they have more leverage they choose to accept scripts that offer them a chance to play against type (usually by obeying the second strategy and turning down every other script that continues their old image).

Hugh Laurie is an example of someone who ended up being so strongly stereotyped as a bumbling comedy character that he felt he had to move to the States to break it. Which he did, playing the straight, less likeable character of House, in the show of the same name. Either way the starting point is your type cast, your brand, so how do you find out what it is?

Firstly, guess. I'd be surprised if as an actor you weren't already aware of the 5-second judgements a stranger might make of you. We usually know our casting. We might even fight against it because we think it's unfair or limiting. You might say things like, "people think I'm a bit posh" or "people assume I'm going to nick their wallet" or "people assume I am easy".

People make snap judgements, and we're not here to discuss the rights and wrongs of that. We are here to use those judgements, those instinctive, rapid judgements, to learn about our brand. If someone has a tattoo we might think one thing, or a posh accent we might assume another, or they have a motorbike, or a toy boy, or fake nails. Each has its own accompanying list of assumptions and judgements.

As an exercise go to a coffee shop and start people watching. Pick a stranger and guess what their name might be.

- What class are they?
- What job do they do?
- Where they might live?
- What might their hobbies be?

It's kind of a fun game. Now can you do it for yourself? What might people assume when you walk into the room. Who will they assume you are? What will they assume you do? Where will they imagine you go on holiday? What income bracket or class would they put you in? In fact, before we make it into the casting suite, judgements have been made on your photo.

When casting directors say that they want you to walk into the room and look like your photo they mean two things. One, literally look like your photo. Don't have a photo that's too glamorous or photoshopped. That's false advertising and will annoy casting directors, as well as waste your time. Two, if your photo sells you as a brand, come in as that brand. The casting director has also 'sold you' as that brand, and it is because you are that brand that you've made it into the room.

For example, I know that sometimes people perceive me as posh, as bossy or pragmatic, sometimes scary, direct or over enthusiastic. These are products of a middle class accent, low authoritative tone, my clothes, my energy, my hair length, and my posture. All manner of data is being automatically read by the observers' unconscious. Once I know I'm going to get cast a certain way I use my photo to tell the casting director that.

If my brand is middle class professional then I ensure I have a headshot of me with a suit jacket on. To be clear, I'm not in costume but the suggestion of authority, the unconscious suggestion of it, is there in the clothing (and hopefully my expression). The casting director wants a lawyer, my headshot – the first impression, snap judgement – suggests lawyer. I then walk in lawyer like, with gravitas and purpose. Even if I don't get the job, the casting director will still be pleased because it looks like they have done their job well.

It's worth saying that part of your job, is not just to get this job, but to think long term; to build relationships with people that last beyond this job onto the next. I have got a lot of repeat work through having good relationships with the people I've worked with. It meant that by the time I had my own role on the West End, as we know, I didn't even audition for it.

You might not be right for this casting or audition, but you want them to like you enough to bear you in mind for next time. Repeat work comes from people liking and trusting you. One way to build like and trust is to take the following business motto: *Your job is to keep your boss's boss off your boss' back.*

How does this relate to acting? In a play, you may protect the director from the producer by being prepared and ready in your understudy role so that an ill actor doesn't stop the show, which costs producers thousands of pounds a night. In a casting, you protect the casting director from his or her boss (which is the director, producer or client) by looking like your photo and by being the brand she has bought. That's why you must be aware of your brand and fulfil it in both headshot and in person. So be aware of your part in the chain, and facilitate.

In my early thirties, my brand for commercials was 'mum'. But let's be more specific, because there are several different types of mum. One extreme casting might be the council estate single mum, fag in hand, swearing at the pram. The other extreme might be the yummy mummy driving the Chelsea tractor.

Yes, it seems like crude stereotypes and clichés. You don't have to be that person (I am not a mum) but television is a fast, visual medium and audiences will want to recognise certain characters immediately. Their dress, accent, the first few words gives the audience this information. It's superficial but it's a fact of life and of the business.

A good friend of mine plays a different brand of mum. With a working class accent, feisty attitude together with a fake tan, false bright pink nails, pink velour tracksuit and bling jewellery. All her business cards (bright pink like her nails) and headshots (feisty expression, hooped earrings) send the same message. She owns this casting bracket 100%. The confidence and clarity of it – and consequently her - are highly appealing and attractive. Does that limit her work? No – that is fear talking. It only stops her wasting her time and casting directors' time, going up for inappropriate parts.

If you are still struggling to think of what your branding is, ask your friends. They might be too close to you and might not want to offend you (or to look like they have judged you), but a good friend will hopefully give you the truth. Or be brave: ask some stranger in the street how old they think you are, what they think you do for a living.

Several things will come up. Don't take it personally because it's not you; it's perception. You could try to fight the stereotype, try to change the world, but you may just lose yourself a lot of work. Acceptance is the key here and knowing. Once we know how we come across we can manipulate it and use it to our advantage.

I realised, in my late twenties, that how I looked didn't reflect fully how people wanted to cast me. I had been a blonde all my life, but my figure didn't fit with the buxom, blonde bimbo type, and my voice was very low so I didn't come across as the naïve, soft Sandra Dee type blonde either.

When I played Lady Macbeth at Edinburgh in 2001 one critic commented with surprise in his review about there being a "blonde Lady Macbeth". Nowhere does Shakespeare ever state what colour hair Lady Macbeth has, or should have, but if you think about it, brunettes are usually cast in the role. Why? Because Lady Macbeth is, on a basic level, seen as evil - so of course, she couldn't be a blonde! Blonde is the hair colour of children and angels. They are identified, on the whole, as being less likely to do evil.[22]

---

[22] In the film, *The Hand That Rocks The Cradle*, the blonde blue-eyed stereotype is reversed to good effect and the angelic blonde is the evil one. This is an exception that played on twisting this very rule.

Singing wise I felt I confused people too. I had this loud, deep contralto voice and being a slim blonde it didn't seem to tally. This could be played to great affect of course, when I did a revue featuring music, scenes and history from European gay culture 1880 to 1930. My contrasting look and voice is what they booked me for. But these were not going to be frequent occurrences. Plus, I also had other practical reasons to want a change, so at 30, I decided to become a brunette.

It was as a brunette not a blonde that I finally got an agent and subsequent theatre roles. I am not suggesting you change anything. I am just explaining how branding can assist our marketing. It is a short cut to explain to others where we fit and consequently how to hire us.

You will already be a strong brand, that's why it's important to discover what it is. What makes you unique? We need to sell that. This is called your unique selling point. Your USP. Whilst one trait might not seem unique, the combination will be. You can't discover and sell what is unique and different about you until you know who people think you are.

Another way to find your branding is to look at the roles you have already been cast in. Can they be grouped together in any identifiable way? And we're not looking for one brand per se, there may be 2-3 but not much more. Yes, they could wig you and you could play anyone anywhere, but until you are a big name, they probably won't.

This book is meant to give you tools to get in the door, then once you are in you can reassess your goals and play with your branding. So, do the exercises in this chapter and write down your two to three possible brands, then ensure your marketing aligns with these.

Another good friend of mine has left the acting industry now, but worked a lot when she was much younger. She was quite a non-conformist in her dress, her hair and her attitude was very bolshie and feisty. Her agent told her to rein all that in. She went into auditions dressed in a regular way, and tried to be regular. But every casting she went into they realised she wasn't the brand they had been sold.

She was lucky people often asked her to read other parts instead, parts that suited her energy. But alongside these there would have been many wasted castings and missed opportunities. She says her one regret is that she didn't own who she was. She was too young to realise that her truer self was a gift. It was her USP.

And it's not just about looks. I had a year where the acting went totally quiet. So I went to the comedy school in Camden and did a course on stand-up comedy culminating in doing a set to friends and family. I then went on and did a few open mics and *The Gong* at the Comedy Store.

Not long afterwards I got an audition for a show that was touring. In the chat, before I read, the director asked me the usual question about what I had been up to. Usually this is just to get a sense of you, to relax you. It shouldn't be a test on what you've been doing acting-wise. After all, they have your CV in front of them.

I explained that things had been quiet so I had gone and done a course in stand-up comedy. After I finished my little chat about that, the director said, "I meant acting-wise, but never mind". I felt really gutted. I thought it had been so much better than saying I hadn't been working. I thought it showed proactivity and courage. Clearly, for that director, it was the wrong answer.

A few weeks later I got the *Little Voice* audition, my first West End audition. I initially wondered if I ought to correct what seemed like the mistake I made in the last audition of talking about my stand up comedy. And then I thought, No! This is what I have been doing and I am proud of it. I believed my gut instinct that told me that the chat / interview part of the audition was to see what kind of person I was. So, I decided to stick to my guns.

The director asked me what I had been up to. Again, I said it had been quiet and though he went to move on, I added, "But then I did a course in stand-up comedy and did a few gigs on the circuit". The whole panel suddenly perked up interested. They started asking me questions, and I shared my experience of *The Gong* and Brighton's Funny Women Festival.

This was the West End audition for *Little Voice*, that as you know, I got. I ended up playing the lead role eight times and it changed my career. I know that they enjoyed my stand-up story. It seemed that they were impressed that I had taken some initiative and they could trust I would understand the comedy of the play.

Also I believe that knowing I had faced the tough world of the Gong Night at the Comedy Store showed them that I would not be afraid to go on in the West End in a lead role, despite fewer rehearsals and less preparation than the principal cast. My script reading put me in the final running, but it is my belief that the stand-up experience guaranteed me that job, I'm sure of it. I was so glad I didn't change my approach, but stayed true to me.

Summary of lessons learnt

- You may be an amazing actor, but you will be asked to play to type first, start there

- Discover what your type is and use it to your advantage

- Make your casting bracket clear and you become more castable

- Be you. Don't try and be a square peg if you're a round one

- Own your journey and your experience, it is your USP

Strategy Eight – Turn pro

Whilst you are an artist, you are also running a business. Sadly, many actors think the industry is not a commercial business but an artistic place of expression and creativity. These actors let their agent do the work. If you are happy to perform for free, forever, then this focus purely on art over business probably won't be a problem. But if you are chasing what I believe to be the dream – doing what you love and getting paid well for it - then you need to take responsibility for your career and run your business like a business.

You may have come from a corporate background and then changed careers, but it's highly likely most actors reading this have never run a business before. With that in mind, let's see how taking a business approach to your career could enhance your success.

Most businesses have seven core business streams. These are:

- Finance

- Human Resources (HR)

- Administration

- Service Delivery

- Learning and Development

- New Business

- Marketing

In a large company different people, even different departments, would cover these roles. As an actor we are responsible for all of them. You are essentially an entrepreneur.

For an actor, *finance* will include keeping invoices and doing your tax return. You can outsource some of this to an accountant and if you are nervous about numbers, I suggest you do this. Thinking about your business finances also means finding a day job that can support your acting career through the quieter times and to pay for tuition, classes or coaching. It is important that you invest in yourself and your business. How will you fund your Spotlight entry, new headshot, show reel or a month off doing the Edinburgh fringe?

Human resources (HR) – Whilst we think it is just us, you may also have an agent, an accountant or even a coach on your team. It is important to outsource the skills you do not have or tasks you cannot do. Your relationship with your agent is key, so I have written a section at the end of the book on agent etiquette to ensure your relationship with your agent is the best it can be.

Administration is all the paper work involved in being an actor: from Spotlight and Equity forms being submitted on time, to organising your diary for auditions, classes and rehearsals etc.

Service delivery involves ensuring you can deliver the promised service. For actors, that service means staying physically and vocally fit enough to do the job (see final chapter on emotional resilience and self-care). It also means we look like our photographs, we have learnt our lines, we are prepared and arrived on time with whatever we need to work.

Learning and Development is everything you do to keep growing as an actor: taking acting classes, learning an instrument or new accent, and working on your personal development to ensure you are moving forward not falling by the wayside.

New Business translates to keeping work flowing through the pipeline. Building relationships is part of this (see Marketing), but mainly it involves auditioning for and applying for work. Which may involve you, your agent or both.

Marketing. I used to confuse marketing with advertising. Marketing is not advertising, but advertising is part of the marketing mix. Marketing is defined as *the process of communicating the value of a product or service to a customer*. So what does that mean to us as actors? It means that if we want people to hire us then they need to first, know we exist and second have a reason to hire us. We must communicate to our customers (directors, casting directors, producers, writers, fans) the value of our product. i.e. the value of us.

What is our value? We know what our brand is now, and so we know what its value is, in terms of uniqueness. Your brand has other values too. For example, your specific value to the Royal Shakespeare Company might be your excellent verse skills or your classical training or the experience you got from the year you spent touring in Twelfth Night. Your specific value to the period drama might be your period look, your ability to ride side-saddle.

Your general value might be that you are talented, represented, reliable, on time, researched, prepared, friendly, you get on with people, you facilitate, you join in. You add value! All things I recommend you do (if you aren't doing them already). Our marketing should communicate to people who we are (our brand) what our value is (our talent, our reliability, our personality).

We communicate our values using marketing tools and tell our clients what to do next. This is called **a call to action**. They've heard *why* they should take an action, (our value) now they need to know which one to take. Look at other companies, what are they selling and how? What is their call to action? Start to be aware of the marketing all around you (branding, USPs, calls to action), and it will educate and reinforce your own understanding. For example, a radio ad might say go online to www.madeupwebsite.com for 10% off your first month's membership. The call to action is to go online. It's not complicated, it's simple and clear. Your call to action might be to go to your website, or to watch your reel, or to go see your play. Tell people what to do, make it easy and quick, and they are more likely to do it.

The Customer Journey

All customers go on a journey before they buy a product. It might look something like this. First, they don't know about the product. Then they hear about it. They (maybe) try it. They like it. They trust it. Then they buy it. In our case, our customer is the casting director, director or producer – and the desired end of the journey is that they hire you.

It is estimated that new customers need to see an advert (or message) seven times before they will act. This number reduces from seven to three, if the message comes from someone we know.

- If a friend recommends a book – you become aware of the book

- When the second friend recommends the same book, we are intrigued

- The third time the same book is recommend by a friend we will most likely buy the book

We can use this information to decide who needs to hear from us at which level of frequency. We may need to contact certain industry contacts seven times before they act. That's why it's important that the marketing is in sync so that each hit is connected and builds on the one before, reinforcing memorability. Others, who know you, are further along the customer journey and need fewer hits before they hire you, or they need a different message. Which stage is your customer at? What do they need next?

With each marketing tool, we must:

- Be clear about the brand, who you are, what you are offering

- Be clear what the value is: uniqueness, general values or specific to that mailing

- Match and sync up with our other materials in terms of the message, style, font colours, logo etc. We want each marketing campaign to take people along the customer journey. Using inconsistent and ever-changing marketing materials seriously diminishes the accumulative impact

- Include a call to action. What they should do next

Here is the full list of marketing materials and how to use them, bearing in mind the four points above.

You!

There is no point having marketing materials that seem to express you are talented, conscientious and a good person to be around if you then turn up to auditions late, or to rehearsal rooms without having bothered to learn your lines. The energy you bring into the room and your attitude is all part of you marketing yourself and telling the customer the values of your product. Don't make them think for a second that your product is arrogant, lazy, unreliable and likely to cause difficulties for the crew. They are unlikely to hire you if they think this, irrespective of how good your website, headshot or audition piece may be. It's like going to the supermarket, whose advert claims they treat customers as their top priority, and then being ignored by the staff. The advert is a waste of money if the reality does not match up to the promise.

Photographs

We've talked a little about photographs and how they might suggest your brand. Try and keep your ego, the one that wants you to look young, sexy or attractive, in check. It's more important that you look like your brand and like you. This may be sexy and attractive, it may not. It will also change with time (sadly!). I turned up to an Internet date once where the guy was much older than his Internet photo. In fact, he was unrecognisable. I wasn't put off by the fact that he had now lost his hair, so much as that I felt he was lying about it. So own your wrinkles, grey hair, large nose or whatever it is. They make up your brand. Of course, you want to look your best in the photograph, as you would at the audition, but keep it real.

On Spotlight and IMDB you can have a range of photos, so use this to show the different brands you offer. Remember, most of the time your photo will be online and probably pretty small, so it needs to catch the casting directors eye whatever its size. Photographers and agents will advise you, and friends may have input, but the key (alongside looking like you and your brand) should be in strong eyes. Strong eyes look directly to camera and make us look back.

Where possible, once you have chosen a strong main headshot use it as much as possible. Use the same photograph on your website and your materials, so that once customers arrive from one to the other the photo immediately indicates that they are in the right place. It matches. When you send a mailing, the matching photos on the postcard will remind the receiver that this is the same person who gave them their business card, or who emailed them an invite to their show, or a link to their reel.

Show reels

Your show reel should be short and punchy. It should showcase you in each of your casting brackets or brands. It must also keep people's interest as long as possible so they can see each of these.

I watched many reels in my time as an agent that made me want to switch off. I am a generous person, but I was bored. So here are some things to avoid.

- *Too long:* Too many people sent in reels that went on and on. Remember, less is more

- *Too Repetitive:* Once I have seen you play a certain character type, we can move on. Every scene should show something new about you

- *Too Confusing:* There were scenes in reels where I wasn't sure who I was supposed to be watching

- *Wrong focus:* There were scenes that showcased a big name actor, and - whilst the intention was to point out they had worked with this level of actor – it rarely showed the actor sending in the reel, in their best light

- *Poor Quality:* Scenes that are too dark, too quiet or too graphic (this latter one is about personal preference, but it is still worth considering)

Remember, when you are going through your raw footage - don't just look for clips where you talk. It's lovely to see reaction stuff too – think Bruce Willis' opening scene in *Pulp Fiction* where he is simply listening. Mesmerising.

Voice reels

These are different in that you are not expected to keep someone's interest all the way through. They can jump about the tracks to find different sounds. But again, think brand. Where were you born, where did you grow up? All these accents will be useful and make up who you are. Ask people which format they would prefer. And on the off chance they want a hard copy, not a link, ensure the reel is not in a black and white case with your photo on it. As someone once told me in a workshop, these tend to look like the order of service for a funeral! Be more imaginative, work with your brand. Could there be an image you can use instead? To portray my posh, low, female London voice, I thought of female legs, in heels, sliding out a black cab. That image implies sexy, posh, female and London, all in one go.

CV

Have a look at your CV or résumé - is it selling you? Be objective. Is it clear and honest? Imagine you receive it with 186 other résumé: does it stand out? Can you find the information you require quickly? In the agency I worked in, we sometimes received convoluted résumés where it was hard to tell which were professional credits and which were drama school roles. It didn't matter necessarily, but we wanted to know. Not being able to work it out is frustrating and makes people give up trying or worse get annoyed with you and think you are concealing something.

Be clear and list your credits as they are because anything else makes you look dishonest or unprofessional. Better to own where you are now, whatever your level, as this will earn you respect from others and opportunities to move on. Clarity is key. If I can't find what I'm looking for in a few seconds – which might be the answer to *do they have experience of classical texts, can they sing?* or *have they done any television?* – I give up. Time is tight for these casting directors, so make their life easier. Make it easier to hire you, and more difficult to add you to the 'No' pile.

Equally, we want you to sell yourself. Don't hide your talents away. If you have a quirky skill add it onto your CV. It can be a conversation point for an audition or might just spark curiosity. I have rapping on my list of skills because I can rap and because it's so contrary to my casting bracket people are often amused by it. I was asked to rap at a theatre audition. Luckily I had a rap that I could pull out of the bag for such an occasion. I didn't get that part, but I know that they a) found it entertaining, b) will remember me and c) that I impressed them by being able to do something on my CV on demand and unprepared.

Furthermore, if a show you were in got an award or Critic's Choice, add a footnote to your résumé saying so. Boost your credibility, wherever possible, as long as it's true. List credits in order of most interesting, challenging or most professional. Why hide your feature film debut under years of other credits just because it happened a few years ago? Finally, less is more. The more skills, accents, and hobbies you have – the less credible they seem. Pick the ones you can do amazingly well, and/or those that you will need for your brand. And make sure you can do any on command.

Covering Letters

I have written (and then as an agent received) many cover letters in my time. My initial letters were professional in content and layout, but they were dull and they were generic. They did not reflect me and they did not make me stand out. By stand out, by the way, I do not mean in the literal sense where you send in your résumé on red paper (not advisable). No, I mean the content of the letter is to the point, passionate and specific. Getting specific requires research. With the Internet there is no excuse now for not knowing who you are writing to, the history of the theatre or show: whatever is relevant.

The letter should be written from the heart, which is easier to do, when instead of mailing 100 letters to everyone in your contacts book, you are writing to the casting director of a show you absolutely love and believe you are right for. When your passion is sincere you won't seem like a generic, self-motivated, suck up. You will show your suitability for the role by experience, skillset, your look or all three. This will look professional and also intelligent. People warm to professional, intelligent, passionate people who are genuine fans of their work. People respond to this.

When I wrote to the National, I explained why I loved the National (sincere flattery), what I had to offer them (my previous understudy experience and a reference from the director of *Little Voice*). I acknowledged in my letter that they got hundreds of letters and made my argument as to why they might take a risk on me (my passion, enthusiasm, work ethic). I also made a joke, to lighten the mood and show some comic flair, about how I'd love to understudy for them but equally I was happy to play a leading role.

When I saw my agent had subbed me for an understudy role, I followed up on my letter, with a postcard to the same casting director. I wrote: *I just wrote to you about understudying and here's the opportunity to hire me.* It was light hearted and short, but it was a reminder. I then saw my agent had subbed me for a<u>nother</u> understudy role, the one I eventually got, but I <u>didn't</u> write to the casting director this time. I dropped a card to the director. As far as the casting director was concerned, my gut told me it was too soon, and would be too much. Be keen, but don't be a stalker!

It transpired that my instincts had been right. When I met the casting director at the audition, I joked that he might have felt a little stalked. He said he got a lot of letters, but mine had really stood out. As I have already told you, I had written letters before, I had worked hard to be original and relevant before. But these new letters came from a different place. I had had my confidence boosted by my new credits but also I was holding my career a little lighter. I was able to write from a place of fun, inspiration, true passion and not fear or desperation. So, learn from my mistakes, no more mass covering letters, save your time.

On a dull practical note: ensure the letter is correctly addressed. Find the casting directors name and ensure it is spelt correctly. My mother worked at the BBC (in Sport, regrettably for me) and she said if any letters came to her with her name spelt wrong (or addressed to Mr!) they went straight in the bin. Deleting an email is even easier. Use the casting director's name. Don't write: *Hi there!* You're not friends (yet!). Also do not write to the casting department, in these financially strapped times there is often not a department, there is one person, so look informed. The same applies to emails. Also note that many CDs work from home. Do not decide – as I did once (oops!) – to take your résumé in person unless you are 100% sure it is an office and not their home address.

Emails

Emails are free. Hurray, no posting costs or stationery costs. But they can look amateur and dull. They may not even get opened. So, how do we improve the odds of them opening your email? One is to put something enticing in the subject box. They will see this regardless unless you go straight into their junk filter for some reason. Write something compelling.

Questions can be good as they are intriguing. If you are mailing about your new reel, the subject could be: *Have you seen this?* Curiosity then gets the better of us. *Seen what?* we think – and then we have to find out! Whereas titling the email: *My New Reel* is dull. Why would we open it? We already know what it is, so we can decide that it's not urgent and we'll look at it later. By this time it's buried and forgotten under the other 100 emails the casting director had to deal with that day.

If you want industry professionals to see your show, you could include an enticing quote from a review in the subject or, the number of stars it got e.g. *The Four Star show you must see next....* Remember if you don't have anything to say other than, "Please can I have job?" then, don't bother. It's not interesting, it's just an ask. As with other mailings, you must be researched, know you are right for a part they are casting, or have something valid and relevant to say.

So you have something relevant to say and you've thought up an enticing subject message, what next? Well you could just write a short professional email, as with the letter, including you signature and any important links. However, if you are mailing a few people you might want to create an email template. Websites like Mailchimp will do a certain amount for free, and you only pay when you want something really fancy. They also have ways to collate email addresses for you, from your website so you can create a mailing list. But remember, it's important to also give people the chance to unsubscribe so you don't annoy him or her, or get reported as a spammer. The email template should look professional and should include links and photographs, a clear message and a clear call to action. No more. It should <u>not</u> be an essay. Casting directors are very busy, make an impact, nudge them to action, and then end!

Also, it's worth noting that casting directors are often freelance and sometimes are out of work, just like actors. Don't send things without knowing if they are working or not. Your mailing may, if they are unemployed, just serve as a painful reminder that they are unemployed as well as being pointless because they're not in a position to call you in for anything. IMDB tells you which casting directors are working on TV and Film, as does watching TV and noting the casting directors down. In addition, there are various websites that discuss projects in the pipeline. Do this work. This is your industry, your market, get educated about who's who.

Silence from them is not the end of the world, the end of the conversation nor can you assume they did or did not watch your reel. Assume neither, because both seem bad. Awful if they didn't bother. Worse if they had bothered and then had nothing to say. Both are just guesses.

Your signature

Not the one you sign but the signature that is at the bottom of emails and letters. It should not only list all the places they can find you, Twitter, IMDB, spotlight, Instagram, Facebook and your website, but the branding fonts and colours should match your hardcopy marketing materials. Plus, if you can, include your headshot in it (not as an attachment, but embedded into the email so they see it instantly). This will add instant recognisability without any action (clicking or downloading) required.

Postcards/ Cards

Postcards and thank you cards are great ways to thank a casting director for an audition or to congratulate them on anything they've done. When I say postcard I don't mean with a view of Brighton Beach or Santa Monica Pier, I mean a postcard you have created with your headshot on it and some news or short bio that sells you. There are many affordable ways to create these mailings.

If you are sending a thank you card or complimenting a casting director on a show they've cast, ensure you've seen it and that the compliment is genuine and specific. Even if you did watch it, a general comment might not seem as genuine as one that picks out a detail and shows you were paying attention. People can smell inauthenticity a mile away and it's a turn off. It insults them, because only an idiot falls for false flattery. So don't do it. And unless you have good reason don't over send postcards. Send them when you have something to say, any more frequently than quarterly might prove annoying. Sometimes you might need to feel this out for yourself. Ask yourself how you would like to be approached. Some people may like frequent contact. Others won't.

Someone I sent a postcard too requested that I email her in the future to save the environment. Make sure you note these kinds of replies and amend your database so you know what they said. Mailing her a postcard again after this reply would look idiotic and would definitely be annoying. Sending her an email, possibly even mentioning something environmentally linked and sincere, might be a good way to open up a conversation, and consequently a relationship. Everyone likes to feel listened to. This is true whether you are communicating in person or electronically.

Business Cards

You are a business; you should have a business card. You never know when you might find yourself in a room with someone who you want to give your details to. You never know when you might walk past someone influential in the street, or someone you're a fan of. You need to have your cards with you so you can facilitate moving the chat or one off opportunity into a more fully-fledged relationship. This is what networking is. Obviously the card should state your Spotlight/IMDB link, your agent, your Facebook, your Twitter, and most importantly your headshot! As an actor our headshot is our calling card. We are cast by what we look like, as well as our talent, so a business card without a photograph is pointless.

If the idea of yourself as a business is still new to you, this may feel awkward. You might feel like others will judge you for having a business card, for promoting yourself, but we have to get away from caring what the other actors may think. Especially as it's more than likely they are envious of your bold statement, they wish they too were as professional. They will probably go home and think about getting their own business cards so you will, in a way, have inspired them.

It seems to be a British phenomenon to find networking or selling yourself as a business to be yucky. It is not arrogant to promote your own business. It is smart. The first time I went out to LA I thought I would state my brand, my USP on my business cards. It was a bold move I would never have dared do in the UK. A producer once described me as 'sexy and funny' so I took that as my USP. I also had a review that had called me 'sizzlingly sexy' so I thought – what the hell. I got business cards with my headshot and website on them, with a tag line saying, "Charlotte Thornton, Sexy and Funny". I'm not really sure how I dared, but I had a limited time in the US to make an impact so I was feeling ballsy. When I handed the card over to people most would read it and laugh, I would then say, "Well, at least I'm half right!" and it broke the ice.

The boldness of this card and some other bold (and by bold I mean out of my comfort zone) actions led to me having lunch with a former producer of *Days of our Lives*. He gave me some fantastic tips on how I might move my career forward. It also, made me confident, that done playfully, we can be bolder than we think.[23]

Good reviews

If you get good reviews, this is great content for your website and social media channels, which we look at further in the next chapter. But they are also great reasons to do a mailing of emails or postcards, especially if the show is still going on. Even if the show is finished it's still a good reason to reach out and remind people who you are and what you're doing. Keep quotes to the point and about you. Generic ones about the show help when you have an invite, but after the show's over, it's not that helpful. Use these quotes in your signature too, whilst they are still fresh, they add credibility to your product and demonstrate value.

---

[23] Though I am not yet convinced Britain is ready for such a full on approach, yet....please prove me wrong and email me your stories!

Recommendations/Testimonials/ Referrals

If someone recommends you, gives you a testimonial, or refers you, this is brilliant. It's proof of the value of your product. Again, think where you can put them? Where is appropriate? I have a good quote from a well-established director that I used in my mailings. I also put it in my Spotlight box (a box above your résumé where you can include current information) and on my website. Another director, at an audition, said I should put the quote on my résumé. Show respect though and ask.

When I asked permission to quote the director who had praised me, he offered me a better, fuller, written quote. I had originally been too afraid to ask in case he took what he had said back (!), but most people genuinely do want to help you. It was another lesson in courage, politeness and mutual respect. The risk had more than paid off because I now had an even better quote, approved by the person I was going to quote on my mailings. In other words, if you are going to use someone's credibility to boost your own, ask.

Press Releases

Each time you are in a show, think about which press might be interested. Big interviews might not happen whilst we are unknown, but local newspapers will always cover the story of *local boy done good*. So, think about adding press releases to your tool kit. A press release is a notice that goes to the press to tell them of a news worthy story. The press release has a set format, which you can look up online. Follow these formats because some publications and websites will dismiss anything they cannot directly put up online. You need an attention-grabbing headline, and you must always include pictures and contact details. As with our cover letters, individually tailored emails to journalists will work better than mass mailings.

I once mentored an actress of dual nationality: Australian, English. Her grandfather had even been a successful actor in Australia. When she had last been to Australia, she had emailed casting directors hoping to use this connection to spark interest and gain a casting. It was a good thought. But there was scope to go further. I suggested that next time she wrote to the press. The press love to do these kinds of stories: the story of the granddaughter following in her famous grandfather's footsteps. This meant we could possibly raise her profile via the press - and then use this as leverage. We know, that being known helps us get seen. It doesn't matter if the casting directors saw the article or not, because my client could email it to them, once it was published.

Gifts

The second time I went to LA, I took a little goody bag for the casting directors I was meeting. It had my reel, résumé and business card in it – plus some English goodies – Harrods tea and shortbread. They loved it. One even stood up and showed it to the class as an example of a great thing to do. This was pleasing but slightly cringe worthy. It was in total contrast compared to what happened when I tried the same thing in the UK with a caster from the BBC.

This time it was a bag with my reel and some Thornton's chocolates in it. Unfortunately I didn't get a chance to offer it to the caster anywhere private. She was exiting the class she taught, but we were all staying on for another teacher. I nearly chickened out, but thought I would feel a fool if I did. So I stopped her as she went past and held out the bag. The caster froze, looked at it suspiciously and asked what it was. The whole room then froze with tension. My arm was frozen too, extended with the goody bag on offer.

The caster refused the bag in no uncertain terms and left the room. It was humiliating. Classes afterwards people would say – *oh yeah, you were the girl who tried to give that caster a goody bag*. Not with malice, just kind of bewilderment. I emailed the casting director afterwards to apologise and explain it wasn't a bribe, it was just to help her remember me, a bit of fun, a bit of marketing. I never got a reply. I assumed I was blacklisted by her, but she did once call me in – and when I said it was nice to meet her again, she looked baffled and said we hadn't met! Take from these stories what you will!

Social media

This is another huge tool for marketing, networking and getting visibility, so the next chapter is dedicated entirely to it.

Marketing is our tool to let people know we exist, who we are and what we do. As you know this is a competitive industry so it's important to get as many of the tools into your marketing toolbox as possible. The key thing is to avoid any generic marketing. You are a specific brand, be specific about what you say and to whom. Be you and you will attract those who like that. There is no point pretending to be something else; you'll end up working with people where the chemistry is wrong, or worse, not working at all because the insincerity has seeped through.

Like life, not everyone will like you. Not because you're doing things wrong but because that is life. We all have a different chemistry with different people and some relationships work and others don't. To a certain extent (as long as you're not being offensive) that's out of your control so don't waste time and energy trying to understand it or fight it. You cannot please all the people all of the time. I believe the same percentage of people will like and dislike you whoever you are, so you may as well be authentic, be you.

And once the marketing is done, be it email, postcard, whatever, **let it go**. Don't wait living in fear at how it was received. Don't use your imagination to create a paranoid story about how they are ignoring you or hate you. Sadly, you probably aren't very high up in their thoughts, or they're busy or away. The truth is that you never know what's going on in someone's life. Don't make it personal. Remember *Strategy One* – don't push.

There is one specific casting director who I had written to at various times in my career because she casts comedy and that was my passion. I sent various interesting emails and letters and cards. Silence. At various times in my role as an agent I called, spoke to her assistants but never got any satisfactory response. Had she seen my reel? Had she read anything I'd sent her (over a long period of time, I wasn't stalking)? I even offered to take her out to lunch; so keen was I to meet this one caster. All of it unanswered.

Then I emailed asking for advice. The email subject was: *Your expert opinion required*. People like to give their opinion. And, it was sincere. I genuinely wanted her opinion. But I was ignored again. I couldn't believe it; it was a yes or no question how did she not have the time! I created a paranoid and narcissistic story in my head about how she must specifically hate me. I must have annoyed her at some point without realising it. I moaned to friends about it in pubs. *One question*, I told them, *it was just one question!*

Two weeks later she responded. She apologised, she'd been on holiday, and she answered my question.

I felt like an idiot.

Learn from my mistakes. When you see yourself or hear yourself building that paranoid story, stop, chuckle to yourself and remember they're human, they're busy and they get a million emails. It really isn't all about you.

Summary of lessons learnt

- It is important to run your business like a business

- Part of the business mindset involves an understanding of marketing and the customer journey

- Building KLT (know, like trust) is key to your acting success

- There are a wealth of marketing tools at your disposal from websites, to reels to press releases

- Ensure your marketing materials match your brand and match each other

- Have a clear and simple call to action

- Make it authentic and individual, no mass or un-researched mailings!

- Assume nothing and don't take it personally

Strategy Nine – Get seen

You are incredibly lucky. You might not think it yet, but you are. I did not have social media or the Internet in my younger years as an actor and it can be invaluable to performers. Why? Because it gives you visibility. You can get known. You can publish video content, reels, songs, and sketches, whatever you want, whenever you want. You don't need to get anyone's permission or approval. Talk about a 100% achievable goal! The platform is there and it's free to use. It doesn't make any difference if you have an agent or not, if you are well connected in the 'real' world or not – here talent and creativity count. Many people have used social media to reach their customers. You can too.

For actors, YouTube, Instagram, Twitter and Facebook are fantastic tools because as well as being free and having a global reach, they're visual (which is great for performers). Furthermore, unlike your website, people are already going to these sites habitually so you are not asking them to make any extra effort. As we have covered, we are in the business of ensuring people know who we are, what we do and where to find us. We have two core social media goals. One is to create a fanbase of people who are interested in and support our careers. The second is to make relationships with people we'd like to work with.[24]

Let's look at the first goal. Building a fanbase may seem unnecessary, arrogant even, but being able to demonstrate a large following gives actors leverage. As we know, producers for theatre or film have to sell tickets in order to survive. Shows that don't sell tickets close down. Consequently actors that can bring an audience with them are more likely to be hired than those who cannot.

Many an actor will bemoan the use of a lesser talented celebrity, for a major show or TV programme. But the producers need to make money and that means bums on seats, a.k.a an audience. An audience guarantees the producers will make money or the TV network will get advertisers. So, we can whine all we like, but it won't change anything. Plus, it shows a lack of understanding of the business side of the industry. The silver lining, courtesy of the Internet, is that producers don't care if you have a high profile from a TV career, a reality show or from attracting fans to a YouTube channel. They just want to know that you will bring in more people than Actor B, and that gives you the edge.

A great way to measure your increasing fanbase is by analysing your social media statistics each month. Keep a simple record on Excel of your follower/like statistics on each of your social media accounts so you can see how they are increasing. When we measure something, we can assess what works, and what doesn't and we also have another way to feel successful.

---

[24] I am indebted to Thérèse Cator for her Social Media Power Player webinar.

It may be in the future that you are going to take this one step further and create your own show or film. You may want to raise capital by crowd funding. How great would it be to already have a fanbase of Twitter followers or Facebook fans that want to see you perform, who want to see you succeed? You can then tweet or reach out to them for help. This is the power of social media: it doesn't care who your parents were or what school you went to. It cares what you tweet and post (your content, your reciprocity, your humour, your branding).

There are many social media sites and new ones pop up every day. I can't discuss them all and you can't be present on them all. So I am going to discuss the big guys i.e. YouTube, Facebook and Twitter in this chapter.

YouTube

Last time I checked, YouTube had over 800 million users and was the third most visited site on the Internet. In terms of visibility, the opportunity here is huge, as artists such as Justin Bieber have discovered. YouTube is a fantastic way to expose your talent, but you will need to be consistent and persistent, if you are going to tackle the fierce competition. YouTube explains that going viral may only create a one-off spike in views so for long-term success you need to look at running a series and a channel rather than just posting a one-off video. YouTube have listed *ten fundamentals* for your YouTube campaign, so go to YouTube to watch that video,

Facebook: Page verse Profiles

If you do have a YouTube channel you will want to publicise your new video blogs (vlogs) on other social media channels. Most people have a profile page on Facebook, so an introduction on how Facebook works may be too simplistic for you, but let's talk through the basics first, so that everyone at every level can get up to speed.

Facebook is a website where many people, such as our possible audience, or directors and casting directors are already hanging out. Having a page or a profile on Facebook is like having a webpage without the hassle of owning and maintaining a website. There are two key parts to having a profile the **wall** and the **newsfeed.**

The *wall* is like a home page: it shows your name, photos, some basic information and anything you post onto your status update. Your status update can include photos, links to websites or videos or just a comments on what you are doing, thinking. This status update then goes onto the **newsfeed** of anyone you have accepted as being your friend. You can turn to your own newsfeed and see posts from all the friends you follow and any **pages** you have **liked** (more on this later).

When someone logs onto their Facebook account they tend to get their newsfeed first, which is a list of things their friends have posted: comments, photos, clips, links, pictures. They can then chose to *like* them (and various other emoticons) by clicking **like** or they can click ***comment*** and say something about their friend's post.

The Facebook newsfeed is not unlike Google, they both rank more frequently visited and updated information higher than others. For Google this refers to websites, for Facebook it relates to the post. The Facebook newsfeed does not default to the 'latest stories' though you can click on this option. Its default is to post what it calls 'top stories', which are the stories of the pages and profiles that are publishing the most interesting content.

How do they decide what's interesting? Well videos and pictures rank higher than words, and frequency of uploading (Facebook loyalty) also raises your ranking. Getting likes (popularity) also raises your ranking. You want to ensure you are updating frequently, with interesting and visual content to keep your fanbase entertained, to gain new fans by existing fans liking your content, and by being higher up in the newsfeed food chain.

Ranking is important because, in terms of the newsfeed, people may only read the top 10 stories. You want your post to be in the top 10. If you have a small amount of marketing budget, why not pay to boost your post with Facebook advertising. You can boost the post you want to increase impressions on, by choosing the particular audience you want to target, and this leads to an increase either in engagement (likes, shares etc.) or increased page likes.

Keep professional with a page

In the arts, friends and colleagues can be blurred. So, the challenge for actors is how do we reflect ourselves honestly to an audience that is both personal and professional. You wouldn't behave the same in an interview or audition as you might with your friends; you would adapt speech and behaviour accordingly. These are our personal profiles and though we need to approve photos we are tagged in, these days, the information shared is still quite personal and a little out of our control. This sometimes clashes with our goal of looking and being professional. So how can we try and be wiser with Facebook to ensure our branding, our marketing message and values remain consistent?

We do this by using our personal profile for close friends and family, and for business we set up a Facebook *page*. A *page* differs from a profile, because it is a one-way information channel. People can join your page by *liking* it, they do not need to know you. You will not get their status updates. Also, and this is key - there is a limit to how many friends you can have on a profile, where as on a page your fanbase can reach millions, and hey you gotta think big. It's a far less intrusive way to keep people up to date with what you are doing. You can't see their newsfeed; they can keep their lives private from you. You can use your page as an extension of your website, as another marketing tool and sync it with you branding.

As with all marketing strategies don't just self promote. It's dull, selfish and a turnoff. So give something back. Add value to people's lives by sharing selected personal bits of information as well as quotes and videos of interest.

So you have your page, how can you get more likes?

- Create interesting content with images, videos and polls. We need to inspire and entertain, whilst sticking to our brand image

- Acknowledge fans (new likes) by giving them a shout out in your status update or by messaging them directly (if you are also friends with them on your personal profile)

- Fans need a reason to support you so make them feel special. Give fans a call to action to go to your website or to like your content. There is now a button you can set up on Facebook for this

- Engage them - Get their opinions by asking them to comment or by using polls

- Express an opinion about something that's taken place in the community / or how you've been helping/working with a charity etc.

At a gig, I had my photograph taken with Harry Styles, just as *One Direction* was exploding globally. For a bit of fun, intrigue and to promote my page, I posted that if I got 100 likes I would post a picture of me with a member of a famous boy band. It was just a bit of fun, but as you can imagine I hit 100 likes and then my 'reveal' post was shared and commented on a lot.

Twitter

Where Facebook has status updates, Twitter has tweets. Where Facebook Pages have Page Likes, Twitter has followers. You can think of Twitter as a compact Facebook. One that only really relies on a newsfeed, of short sentences: 140 characters to be precise. That is why it's often called a micro-blogging site.

Twitter is a much briefer version of Facebook but don't underestimate its potential. Unlike Facebook, Twitter enables you to reach out to people you don't know. Facebook will block you for this. You can reach out by following anyone you want on Twitter, they may or may not follow you back. And you can reach out by contributing to conversation boards, where new people might follow you based on what you say or tweet. More on these later.

So Twitter basics: You can have a picture on your own wall, but you can't write much about yourself. So, think carefully about what you write, and what picture you use. As usual, think about your brand. Are you syncing it up with your other marketing in style and photo? Are the few words you get to describe yourself selling you and promoting you? Do they include a link to your website?

Twitter has its own newsfeed called a Twitter feed. Here you will see the status updates or tweets from anyone you follow. Unlike the Facebook newsfeed this isn't ranked, this is in chronological order, starting with the most recent tweet down. The tweets are much shorter than Facebook status updates, but they can still include photos, videos and links to other sites. Instead of having *friends* you have followers.

You can find people to follow if you know their twitter address, called a **Twitter handle,** it begins with an @ sign. Or if you don't know their handle, type them into the search box and see if you can find them. Then when you do, simply click the button called **Follow** and it will then go green and say *following.* When someone follows you, you will get an email telling you, **you have a new follower on twitter.**

To compose a tweet there is an icon with a quill on it. If you tweet a message it will go out to your followers. i.e. those who follow you, not to those you follow. But if you put a twitter handle in the tweet e.g. hello @charliethornton that person will get a message saying **someone mentioned you on twitter** and a link to see what you wrote. I will get this even if I am not following you. If you follow someone who follows you back then you can also send direct messages (DMs) which are private and do not go on anyone's newsfeed.

To find new people to follow, you can use the search box, or see the suggestions Twitter is posting on the main page – usually based on what Twitter thinks you want. Or you can look at a company or person, and see who is following them. Obviously, a company or person relevant to the acting industry i.e. an agent, director, actor etc. Follow as many people as you like, because you can put them into lists later so that you haven't got a newsfeed overloaded with tweets. But either way, don't expect to read every tweet. There are millions. You can always go to someone's specific page if you want to see what they have tweeted about most recently.

As I mentioned earlier, unlike Facebook, Twitter newsfeeds are just listed in order of chronology so you see the most recent, not the 'most important' first. Aside each post it says when it was tweeted 1m (one minute ago) or 2h (two hours), 3d (3 days) etc. The way to 'like' a tweet on twitter is to retweet it or favourite it. You **retweet** by hitting the retweet button, often two arrows chasing each other. You can see where a retweet has occurred in the newsfeed because it has **RT** for retweet in front of it or it says below **retweeted by @charliethornton**.

Unlike 'liking' content on Facebook, 'retweeting' sends the tweet from your newsfeed onto the newsfeed of your followers. So, if I tweet something to my 200 followers and one of them retweets it to his 150 followers, not only has my tweet got the potential of having been seen by 350 people (350 impressions) instead of my 200, but also someone on the new 150 list might like or agree with my comment so much that they decide to follow me and my fanbase goes from 200 to 201. Sounds trivial but hopefully you see the compound potential: many drops make a waterfall. The possibility for both growing your fanbase and exponentially increasing your reach is huge.

Your tweets should not look like a list of status updates: *I just ate some cake!* Or *here's me on my flight to Spain,* they should include either a twitter handle @ or they should include a # (hashtag). The # sign takes you to a conversation board, that <u>anyone</u> can join in if they include that # in their tweet. You can create your own conversation board by putting # in front of anything you like. But it might not catch on, unless you have lots of followers.

Is a brilliant way to find and engage new followers. You might want to use #Actors to engage actors or #Auditions to share news or advice. Or you might want to comment on a programme you are watching. E.g. *Loved Sharon's last comment on #xfactor.* If you go onto twitter whilst *The X Factor* is on you can go onto #xfactor and engage with the audience that shares that interest. You can really get involved. You could add comments of your own, which (ensuring you include the # conversation in your tweet) might get retweeted by strangers reading that conversation or you can retweet funny content from others which you think will amuse your own fans.

It's worth adding – make sure you **review** the hashtag you create. The last thing you want is for it to be misinterpreted and to go viral for all the wrong reasons. A prime example was Susan Boyle's Album party #susanalbumparty.

When you go onto Twitter there is a list telling you what subjects are trending and so you can jump in on popular conversations, or look at your newsfeed and see which ones your friends, work colleagues or aspirational groups (those you want to be working with) are talking about. Then you can add value. Tweets without @ or # will not develop your influence or increase your fanbase.

It's also important to reciprocate, retweet and like other people's content. Carve out time to do this each day. Support other people, plug their shows, and laugh at their jokes. All successful people know that **you must give before you get** and people who live fulfilled lives are usually those who give the most. Don't do it willy nilly, but when it is sincere and authentic. I always give shout outs (retweets, likes) to acting friends in shows, or when they've posted reviews, or when someone asks for a retweet or a casting director has gone to Twitter to source a really niche role that they are struggling with. This is how relationships work, give and take. So support, listen, help and share. Online or offline, it's still all people. Pay it forward!

Here are some ways to be generous on Twitter.

- Retweet someone's show or review

- Retweet anything you like that might help people or make that twitter user feel loved

- Always reply to new followers thanking them. You can automate this

- Recommended others follow them – use #ff on a Friday – FF means Follow Friday to recommend people to follow. You can find other people to follow this way too.

- If anyone tweets, writes a review or congratulates you for something, take the time to reply, thanking them for the shout out. This will create conversations and help strengthen your relationship with fans

Example

I follow several casting directors. I saw one had posted a plug of a Television show she'd cast. If I were short on time I would have just retweeted it for her, as a shout out. But I had time, so I watched it online then retweeted it with a comment stating what I had liked about the show. It was genuine. That casting director will then get an email saying, "someone mentioned you on twitter" and hopefully she will be pleased someone saw and liked her show. Another casting director tweeted about getting a place on the London Marathon. I did the marathon a few years ago so I retweeted his tweet with a comment congratulating him and saying how fun the marathon is. Note that, I am not asking for parts. I am getting involved in their conversations using the @ and # symbols.

This may seem trivial again, but it's a way to build relationships through shared interests, rather than asking for work. When you have good relationships with people getting the work or audition is easier; they already know you, hopefully they already like you or perceive that they do. Or maybe it's just that from the odd tweet, your face has become familiar to them, and they can't explain why but they feel that they already like or trust you. This is how you can start to build relationships as well as a fanbase. To be clear these were all genuine. I don't pretend I support Arsenal or like fly-fishing. That's just lying, I wouldn't fake that in person, so I'm not going to fake it online.

For further info follow @twitterbusiness for tips and advice.

Instagram

You may also want to use Instagram or Snapchat. The audience on here is a lot younger than on Twitter and Facebook, so think which customer you might be targeting on these platforms. Again, the same social media rules apply. Be generous with likes, replies and shout-outs. Post frequently. Use stunning imagery. Use hashtags to take you beyond your followers to gain new ones.

Time Management

Social media requires you to be consistent and persistent. This can be a huge drain on your time and resources. Create a daily routine where you set a limited amount of time to check your feed, so it doesn't distract from your other career priorities. Use resources such as Buffer, TweetDeck or Hootsuite to automate social media posts and share content. Set aside one day a week to film several YouTube videos in one go, or to write a weekly blog. As with all goals, small daily steps achieve more than random bursts of activity followed by silence.

Websites

Another place where you can be creative and visible is on your own website. If you don't have a website yet, it's time you did. I'm not a web designer or coding expert, but these days a basic site will require you to be neither. However, if you are nervous – as with the accounting – then outsource this to an expert or a friend. It may be a friend or someone who might swap some of your knowledge for some of theirs. Or you may feel computer savvy enough to do it yourself using a book. I use Word Press, which is one of the most common because its basic templates are free and they are easy to use.

If you do have a website, the content should sync with your other marketing material. Do they match in terms of your headshots, fonts, colours and brand values? Are you keeping it up to date with interesting new information? If not, Google will not rank it highly, which means that when someone searches for your name in Google many websites may come up before yours. You want your website to be in the top three otherwise no one will find it. Equally, without posting new information onto your site regularly, those that do visit it will have no reason to return.

Your website can be kept fresh with new information (to increase its search engine optimisation (SEO)) simply by writing a blog.[25] Writing a weekly or bi-weekly blog talking about your acting career, your life, something in the news, plays you've seen, your passion for sitcoms, kiwi fruit, European churches or whatever your interests are. This has two benefits. One it will give you a creative output over which you have control (which can be a real boost in the often frustrating world of being an actor), and two, it will rank your website higher in Google. If writing isn't your thing then do a video blog.

Your website is also the ideal place to have a page where you collect the email addresses of your fans. Having a contact database of your fans means that you have control and can market specifically to them. This may not seem massively relevant now, but it is important to grow this fanbase, and have their details so that you can inform them of what you are up to, via a direct newsletter. So even if they don't go to your site or follow your blog on their RSS feed, they will know what you are up to.[26] They will feel more and more connected to you and your success. They will come and support you in shows and this means you can demonstrate box office draw to producers. You have a fanbase PLUS you are in control of it. It might seem nothing now, when there may only be your six best friends and your mum on the list, but you can grow this list with clever marketing and it will then give you leverage.

Finally, a word about attitude. Online your words can be retweeted and liked and passed on and seen by people you might never imagine would or could see them – and for years after, even if you try and remove them. Great if you are out in the online world being positive and contributing. Not so good if you are bitching about the bad audition you had or the casting director who hasn't responded to your mailings. You're burning bridges. I am stunned how many times casting directors and directors feel the need to advise actors not to bitch online or at auditions.

---

[25] Google uses something called spiders that trawl the web and decide which websites to list for each search made, and in which order. So if you do a search for your website or name, you will see how good your SEO is. Are you ranked in the top three? Ignore the very first three, as these are advertisers who have paid to be at the top. The rest of the search is called the organic search and this is what we can influence by increasing our SEO with tools such as keywords and fresh content.

[26] RSS stands for really simple syndication and means that someone can click on RSS on your feed and get an automatic notice that you've written a new blog, without having to return to your website.

More amazingly are those who have told me actors email or tweet them directly to complain that they have been ignored. How stupid are these actors?! It can be hugely frustrating, believe me I've been there. And yes it is sometimes unfair, and we can be mistreated, but have your tantrum privately.[27] In the real world, be a pro. That means being a grown up and accepting that it's not all abut you. Casting directors are busy doing their jobs, they get inundated, don't be so rude that they black list you. And not just you, possibly your agent as well. And not just that casting director but every other casting director they are friends with will get to hear about it. It's just not smart! So don't do it, you are giving actors a bad name and losing yourself work.

Summary of lessons learnt

- YouTube can generate visibility and we have creative control

- Using social media you can grow a fanbase

- A fanbase gives you leverage and power

- Social media is a fantastic and free way to gain visibility

- Share your talents on social media to increase chances of being known

- Consider your brand on social media and keep personal and professional separate where possible

- Be generous, contribute, don't simply ask or vent

- Make time every day to be consistent about your social media marketing

- Don't put anything online that you wouldn't want attributed to you and printed in the National newspapers

---

[27] If you are actually abused in any way, then contact the appropriate person or body, such as Equity and make an official complaint.

Strategy Ten – Build emotional resilience

Actors and artists are often sensitive creatures. Even if we aren't, the brutality of an industry where rejection is a continual part of the process, can wear anyone down. Knowing that we are going to have to take some knocks throughout our journey, it is worth creating a strategy so that we can, not only get back up, but also get back up quickly. That strategy is to build emotional resilience.

Emotional resilience (ER) is not something we practise as and when we need to. ER is a foundation that we build from day one and then maintain, so that it is there when we need it. You can wait until you are sick before you eat healthily, exercise or manage your stress, but it is more effective if you start right, from the beginning. So how do we build up our emotional resilience? Here are some practical things you can do, as well as some topics for further exploration.

The Journal

The journal, for me, is the main foundation of ER and is inspired by having seen the benefits of my own gratitude journal and then learning about creating happiness from author Shawn Achor, *The Happiness Advantage*. Writing in this journal is going to form part of your daily routine, so buy a beautiful book and commit to this process. It may seem at first glance to be trivial but throughout this chapter its importance will become clear.

In the journal you will write:

- Three things you are grateful for every day

- A daily act of random kindness

- One step you are going to take towards your goal today

You may also want to use the journal to note down your successes and to record the proof of your new beliefs, as discussed in *Strategy Five*.

Gratitude

"I cried because I had no shoes until I met a man who had no feet." Helen Keller.

As we explored in the Law of Attraction, gratitude is a powerful emotional state. We want to get into this state daily and maintain it. The old fashioned trick of counting your blessings sounds out-dated and a bit trite; especially if you have your negative lenses still on and think you don't have any blessings. But believe me, this habit will shift you from negative to positive 95% of the time.[28] In your journal write down everything you have to be grateful for: from your family, to your health, to every lucky break you've had. The fact that you have grown up in a country where you can even dare to dream to be an actor is a hugely lucky thing. Many people would never dare dream that dream, they may never even have seen a television. Their life is about survival.

There are always things to be grateful for. Make your list. Feel the gratitude each day by reading the list and adding something new to it. It needs to be done daily, because that is how habits form. It is believed that habits take between 30–60 days to stick, and the old habits won't want to go easily, so do this every day. This will cultivate what coaches call the *attitude of gratitude*.

RAKs (Random Acts of Kindness)

To enhance our happiness further we are going to do a daily RAK. This may just happen organically, for example, you help an old lady cross the road, but Achor suggests that conscious acts (i.e. deliberate ones) have more power. These can be brought about by thinking, *who can I help today?* It may simply mean texting a friend who is going through a tough time, calling a relative, or paying someone a genuine compliment. RAKs make us happy, which we now know is the precursor to success. Happiness also has a high vibration.

Small Daily Steps

The final part of the journaling process is to write down the one thing you are going to do that day to take you towards your objective. This shapes your brain to look for opportunities and gets you in the daily habit of moving towards your goal. As we have explored, it is the consistency and persistence that pays off in the long run. However small, write down one thing you could do today and then go do it!

---

[28] I want to add here, that if you do have any serious issues with feeling negative, low, depressed or anxious, then I highly recommend finding a professional counsellor or therapist. I am not qualified to deal with those serious issues, nor is this book the place.

Self-care

Self-care has various parts to it. One is physically taking care of yourself through healthy diet and exercise. There is a wealth of resources on this topic, so I am not going to go into it further. But suffice to say that being an actor is a physically demanding job, so being fit and healthy helps. I once had a big night, two nights before I was due to film an advert. I woke up early for the filming and realised I had barely any voice.

I was in a total panic about how unprofessional this would appear, and that the advert might have to be cancelled due to my inability to perform. Fortunately some water, steaming and playing a relaxation audio in the car to the studios meant I arrived with my voice. But it was nearly a self-inflicted disaster. We all like to let loose every now and then, but keeping healthy means you won't suddenly find that you have lost your voice, just as that key audition comes in.

Stress

What's often overlooked with our self-care is our emotional self-care. Stress might feel emotional but it causes physical symptoms. In fact, 90% of all doctor visits are attributed to issues brought about by stress. Stress causes disease. When we are stressed we are in fight or flight, we are not in repair, or digest, or create. For actors, removing stress is key to our health, our well-being and our creative ability.

I had issues with stress when I was in my twenties, and stress for me meant cold sores. No actor wants to go to an audition with a cold sore, or mouth ulcers. They could stop you getting work. They certainly stop you looking and sounding your best. Thinking positively, meditating, taking time out in nature, are all antidotes to stress. But let's look at some of the ways we cause our own stress, and consequently, lower our emotional resilience in the first place.

Judgement

We assume that most people think the same way that we do. This is not true, but we think it none-the-less. As a consequence, how we think affects what we believe others think about us. Let me simplify with an example. If you judge people who dye their hair, you will be unable to dye your hair without imagining that you too are being judged. Some people won't judge whether you dye your hair or not. They might find something else to judge you on instead. Trying to second guess what that might be, and correct it ahead of time, is as pointless and unachievable as a dog chasing its tail. And a giant waste of energy too.

Worrying what others think about us, and feeling judged, holds us back from achieving what we want to achieve. Not only will the world be a kinder place without all the judgements, but also the world inside your head will be calmer. Judging others, and ourselves, is a habit that simply needs to be broken. When you hear yourself have a judgement about someone else, say the word *delete* in your head. As you stop judging others, you will feel less judged yourself and more loved.

Perfectionism

Perfectionism (judgement's twin) is our strategy to keep us safe from judgement. We believe that if we can be perfect, then no one can judge us. But perfection doesn't exist. Being human sometimes means slipping up, failing, having a bad hair day, and accidentally saying something stupid. When people pretend to be perfect it disconnects them from those around them, which causes us immense emotional pain. Inspire others, not by being perfect but by showing your humanity, your vulnerability, your mistakes and how you handled them.

As well as being a continuous stress and energy drain, perfectionism also stops us moving forward. We can't take the required action until it is perfect or we are perfect, and it (or we) never is. Go for completion, not perfection to avoid putting things off. Anyone who does judge has their own issues (see above) and we need not waste time on their (usually unwanted and unsolicited) opinions. As we release our own judgements we learn to release the need to be perfect.

As Brené Brown writes, in *Daring Greatly*, "For some folks, perfectionism may only appear when they are feeling particularly vulnerable. For others, perfectionism is compulsive, chronic, and debilitating – it looks and feels like an addiction. Regardless of where we are on this continuum, if we want freedom from perfectionism, we have to make the long journey from "What will people think?" to "I am enough."." I am enough, would make a wonderful affirmation to add to your pre-sleep routine, as discussed in *Strategy Four*.

Comparisons

There is no joy, no learning, and therefore no point, in comparing ourselves to others. The path is not linear, so someone who looks ahead today can be behind (if there were such a thing) next year. You might feel that due to certain circumstances you are crawling whilst others seem to be shooting forwards in their careers. But then someone might offer you a lift in their metaphorical car, and you'll overtake, for a time or not – who knows?

It's so easy to look at others and wish we had what they have. But if we'd come along a different path we would have missed out on the friends we met along our way and the lessons that stretched us into the champions we now are. As we looked at in *Strategy Two*, envy can be used to guide us on what our true vision looks like. Take it as a helpful indication to move towards that vision, then let the emotion go. Simply look at the person you envy and say, "Oh yes, I want that for me too". Thank them, for helping you get that clarity, then move your energy back to <u>your</u> plan. To progress rather than digress, don't compare yourself with anyone other than yourself.

Taking it personally

It can be hard not take it personally when we do not get the part. Especially as we often have no idea why. This leaves us to our paranoia and limiting beliefs that tell us it was because we were not good enough. But whatever we imagine is simply a guess. This list was given to me by the TVI actors' studio, in LA (where I attended several boot camps). It is a list of more likely reasons why you didn't get the job. Before you default to imagining you weren't good enough or worthy enough – read these:

- Although you did a great audition and dressed the part, you naturally did not have the right look. There is nothing you can do about that

- You had the right look, did a great audition, however you were not a match with the other person (or people) that have already been cast, or that are more important for the piece

- The ad agency changed their mind creatively (this happens a lot) and went in a different direction. Note: I saw an advert on TV that I had auditioned for and not got. The 'presenter' I had auditioned for was now *male*. No matter how good an audition I'd done, that was a direction change I could not have adapted to!

- They are still shooting the campaign but the specific commercial you auditioned for was canned. I once booked a job that was then canned less than 24 hours before I was due on set

- You got down to the final two. Everyone acknowledged you could do the job brilliantly, but the other person just had a slight something extra that tipped the scale in his or her favour

So, if you are going to guess the reason why you didn't get it – pick one of the above, rather than picking yourself apart. Equally don't swing to the other extreme, where you take a privileged stance, stating you **should** have got that role, as if you are somehow more deserving than any of the rest of us. You are no more, nor are you less, worthy than anyone else.

Meditation and Mindfulness

Again, there is a wealth of resources on both of these topics, so explore. The overall theme is to find time to be present and to take back control over the monkey chatter in our heads. This removes stress, creates more peace in our worlds, and the benefits include making us healthier and even smarter. There are many apps to help you (such as Headspace) and like anything, it simply takes commitment and practice. As we looked at briefly in *Strategy Four*, meditation also helps slow our brain waves down into a state more conducive to adopting new beliefs.

Tapping

Tapping, also known as EFT (Emotional Freedom Technique), is a way of releasing negative and trapped emotions or beliefs. Various acupressure points are tapped on, in a set order and with key phrases, to bring the emotion into the body and then release it. There are a lot of videos online showing you how to do this, it is free and you can do it anywhere at anytime. Former actor, and EFT expert, Brad Yates, is especially clear and helpful, whilst also retaining a wonderful sense of humour. I recommend you check out his website and YouTube videos.

Have it now

It is empowering not having to wait for things to happen, but to take back control and create what you want now. Creating the experience now is about using your own creativity, imagination and resources to create the experience of having your goal before you have achieved it. Mostly what we want from life is not money, or fame, or everlasting youth, but the experiences we believe those things can bring. If we understand that more than the goal, we want the experiences it can bring, we can take back some power by creating those experiences for ourselves now, without having the need for the goal to be fully achieved. Paradoxically, according to the Law of Attraction this will also help manifest the goal.

Look back at the objectives you wrote down for yourself, from *Strategy Two*. Ask yourself, what is your desired outcome of achieving your goal? Under each goal is another, more real goal. We might not want the fame, we want recognition or to have achieved something challenging. Take some time to explore what is really underneath your goals by asking *why* you want them. It might be a desire to be seen, to be loved, to feel like you matter, to make an impact or to contribute. Then brainstorm how you can achieve the same experience without achieving the goal itself.

For example, my objective was to get a role on television. The desired outcomes were to gain recognition and exposure. The desired experiences were to feel happy, excited, and hopeful. So now I can look at this and brainstorm how I might achieve these things on my own.

With the desired outcome to gain more influence my brainstorm looked like this:

- I could write a blog and start creating a fanbase using social media

- I could increase my visibility by filming my own sketches for my website and put them on YouTube

- I could get some new really stand-out headshots

- I could do a crazy stunt for the media

- I could advertise

- I could write my own film, like Matt Damon and Ben Affleck

- I could put on my own production and draw attention to it by having a high profile person in it

- I could see if any of my contacts would refer me

The desired experiences can also be achieved, which were: to feel happy, hopeful and successful. How might I create that? It might be something simple: the hope gained from sending a letter out, the happiness from doing something fun and playful or the success of achieving a daily goal.

Doing something good for yourself fills you up with an energy that makes you a better person in the world. Go do something right now on your list that makes you feel closer to achieving your goal, by experiencing a taster of the same results the goal would bring. Don't wait until everything is how you want it to be, because most of life is a process and nothing is ever complete.

Be creative

Sometimes the underlying desire behind your visions is simply to express and create. We are all creators. Artists and musicians can create whether they are in work or not. For actors, it can be harder. Look for other ways to be creative and to express. It might be through poems, song writing, baking, crafts, music or singing. It doesn't matter. The point is to take responsibility for your creative needs and not to abdicate this pleasure and need to the industry alone. If your needs are filled you will be less needy and desperate, which is attractive. You will also keep those creative juices flowing between jobs. These all contribute to your ability to stay in the game and overcome any obstacles, and to your well-being.

Finally, change your perspective. Of course, when we don't get certain jobs – which we really wanted, or that agent doesn't sign us, it can knock us down. We may need a little time to lick our wounds. My advice is to allow yourself time to wallow, but set a deadline, a time limit. Don't stay too long at the pity party. Then, most importantly, get back up!

I found it helpful to imagine my life was a film, and this was the part where the hero gets knocked down. This was simply an obstacle that had to be overcome, that made the narrative more interesting, the final victory more satisfying. I was not at the end of the film, because the film never ends with the hero failing. The film ends when the hero has succeeded. This setback does not define you. Remember that it is simply that part in the film where the hero has to dust themselves off and persist.

Summary of lessons learnt

- Start a daily journal of gratitude, RAKs and a daily goal

- Nurture yourself

- Stop judging yourself and others

- Aim for strong human, not exhausted perfectionist

- Don't compare yourselves with others

- Don't take it personally

- Meditation, mindfulness and tapping are helpful tools for ER

- Have what you want now

- Get creative and express yourself

- It isn't over until you say it is

Congratulations

We are now at the end of the book. I congratulate you for investing in yourself; for taking the time to ensure that you give your career and your dream everything you can. If you action even a few of these strategies you will have an advantage. Well done for taking responsibility for your journey and arming yourself with expertise!

There will still be other injustices and rejections and disappointments on the road – the bumps – but remember that this is true for anyone on the path to success, whatever the goal. It's not the end of the road, until you decide it is.

Stay in touch; let me know how you get on. You can interact with me via my website, blog or YouTube channel. I want to hear your questions, your success stories and what inspires you.

Go out there and do it. Make a schedule, make a plan, then take those daily steps towards success, consistently, persistently and with all the self-care and self-love you deserve. Whatever happens life is an adventure. For those who dare to follow their dreams there will always be rewards; even if they don't initially look like the ones we were anticipating.

Good luck, break a leg and go do it!

Bonus Chapter - Craft and Etiquette

I just want to talk a little bit about craft and etiquette, because some people leave drama school seemingly unaware that there is a way to behave that will get them work and there is a way that won't. But aside from that selfish objective of getting work, I think it creates a better world if we don't act like the egocentric, selfish divas actors are sometimes depicted to be. So, learn some etiquette and behave like a pro (even when other so-called professionals around you are not).

Learn your lines. You might think it's your prerogative when you learn your lines, especially if it seems to you (though that doesn't mean it's true) that the director or assistant director is relaxed about it. The etiquette is that you're off book (you've learned your lines) by week two. Remembering lines is acting 101 and though it can be tedious, and get harder as you get older, the work has to be put in. Like athletes training for hours a day, actors must learn to put in the hours. It affects the whole cast when you don't know your lines. They can't act with you properly when you're holding a script. They get used to working with your misspoken lines. Having an acting job is a very privileged position, and many really hard-working actors would love to take your place. So show some gratitude for the job and your respect for the cast by learning your lines.

I have further tips on learning lines on my website and YouTube channel.

Be on Time. If you've bought this book it's because you desperately want to succeed, don't you? So, give it 100% and be on time. No, be early. Warm-up, or socialise, or get that coffee. But there is nothing worse than other people busting a gut to get there on time, only to sit around waiting for you. Why should they? Our job is time-precious. In the theatre, the curtain goes up at 7.30pm. There is no flexi time. Being late, like not learning lines, looks lazy and disrespectful to the rest of the cast and crew, with whom I would hope you'd like to be making good relationships with.

Rehearsal room etiquette. Don't enter or re-enter the room when someone is mid scene. This is a total no no. People are juggling lines and blocking whilst trying to be in the moment, they don't need your bumbling entrance into the room, no matter how quiet. Stick your ear to the door and wait patiently until you can hear the scene is over.

Cast and crew. Theatre, film and television are all group efforts. I personally love working in a team. I have done stand-up but I much prefer being within the company of The Company. But there are still some old school actors upholding some sort of hierarchy by sucking up to the supposed 'stars' and looking down on the newer actors or those in smaller roles. There are producers guilty of continuing this too. I don't care how many lines you have, everyone counts, including the stage management team and the crew. Treat everyone equally and with respect. It's really closed minded and blind sighted to assume you should only mix with your perceived level. A level which, in the arts, can change month to month.

Sometimes it seems that actors are only interested in befriending those who can help them. This is false and ignorant. It's ignorant because you have no real idea. The actor you're ignoring today may be a casting director tomorrow, or be related to an influential director/writer/producer. You just don't know. The industry is small and people talk. I'd hate for them to be talking about you, behind your back, about things you were unaware of, such as rehearsal room etiquette or when to learn your lines. But even worse, if you're creating issues yourself; by being unable to leave your annoyances, or lack of chemistry with other people, at the door. Take the issue as a challenge, not something to win and bitch about with your friends, but one to overcome. Learning to work with people different to ourselves helps us grow. The more you grow as a person, the more fulfilling your life will be and in all likelihood the better an actor you'll become.

Agent Etiquette. If you don't trust your agent to work with you (not for you) then you shouldn't sign with them. If you do trust them, then let them do their job. You could decide that they work for you, and choose to be demanding: "Come and see me in this, put me up for this, why haven't I had an audition in ages." But the reality is, unless you book work, they are working for you for <u>free.</u>

It's much better to think of it as a collaboration. How can you help each other? So before you ask what has your agent done for you, ask what have you done for your agent? Are you helping them get you work by being on time and by being prepared? Do you have all your marketing materials organised? There is no point blaming your agent for a lack of auditions when it is you who hasn't yet got a show reel. As this book has shown you, there are many areas where you can be in control and make proactive efforts to be known and succeed. Make sure you are doing these before you waste your agent's valuable time.

It's so easy to sit at home thinking, *I'm getting no auditions so my agent must have forgotten about me, be slack, unconnected or incompetent.* There are so many other factors. When I worked in an agency I saw that sometimes the lack of auditions was due to budget issues (recession, arts cuts), or simply the challenge of competing with higher profile agents and higher profile actors. A lack of auditions does not mean a lazy agent.

Before you sign with an agent, ensure you trust them and that you are both on the same page about where your career is heading, and the type of work that you would like to do. For example, don't sign with a musical theatre agent if you have decided you want to pursue straight acting. At this initial meeting, though you are nervous and possibly desperate for them to represent you, you must hold back and ensure you ask your questions. *Who do they know? How can they help you?* For it to be a good fit, the vision and the chemistry must be right. Then you can trust them to do their job and you go do yours.

Every now and then agents do culls. This means they drop actors from their books like a company letting go of staff. They have to. And don't think this is purely based on who is bringing in the money. A personal management agency which I was represented by did a cull. I was saved, not because I had brought in any money, but because the team liked me. My experience as an agent had given me the insight and understanding of the agent's role. It impacted how I behaved. I was always appreciative of an audition, no matter how last minute. I told them when I wasn't free well in advance. I spoke to them courteously and, where possible, supported and networked with their other clients. I didn't hassle them, but I was available. I was interested in what they were doing, as well as what I was doing.

Keep developing your talent. As we looked at in *Strategy One*, Malcolm Gladwell's research indicates that it takes 10,000 hours to be brilliant. So get as much experience as you can. I have toured old people's homes, and though it wasn't glamorous, it was fun and I learnt a lot. A person coughing in the audience puts off other actors easily but, when you've performed to all kinds of audience in all kinds of venues, you aren't so easily fazed. It also taught me that it's the audience that counts, whether they are in an established venue or not is an ego thing and we need to keep that in check.

I also did ten years on the fringe (that's off Broadway for those Americans reading) and again I just learnt masses. There were times when I felt frustrated about how slowly my career was progressing. But what it meant, in retrospect, was that by the time I was in the West End, in a massively challenging role, I hit the ground running. I was ready. It's arrogant to assume you're so good you don't need to learn anything.

In LA, actors always go to classes. They constantly keep working on scripts and networking with casting directors. Even actors in successful soaps spend an evening a week or a month studying. It's a culture that is starting to be adopted over here in England too. If you are a professional you should welcome the opportunity to keep learning, growing and to refine your art.

Finally, be aware of how you come across. It can make the difference between people hiring you again or not. Constantly think, how can I add value? And then go do it!

Acknowledgements

Success is never a solo event. It's all about collaboration and the team we have around us. With that in mind, I would like to sincerely thank all my friends and family for their support throughout my career, and my husband's support whilst I wrote this book.

It also wouldn't have been possible without my mentors and guides, Dallas Travers, Janet Kells, Jeev Sahoo and Kylie Fitzpatrick. I want to thank Denmark Street Management for signing me and for being an amazing (and entertaining) place to learn about the industry. Also to Shepperd-Fox.

Thank you to those who helped me get this book into (hopefully) a decent shape and get it out there: Richard Burgess, Pat Thornton, Will Thornton, Andy Smith, Natalie Waghorn Brodie, Juliette Carrington, Joanna Benn, Jenny Gallacher, Wendy Miles, Rosa Huynh, Asha Mistry, Katie Ashworth, Mal Koffman, Caroline Dore and James Carter. To Brad Yates for his videos and workshops. To Thérèse Cator for everything she taught me about social media.

And finally, thank you for buying this book. I cannot wait to hear about your journey!

Bibliography

I have read so many books over the years, which will have influenced what I have written, but that I won't remember. However, here are those that I have quoted or that will be useful to you for further reading.

About Acting – Peter Barkworth

Creative Visualisation – Shakti Gawain

Daring Greatly – Brené Brown

Do the Work – Steven Pressfield

How to be a Happy Actor in a Challenging Business – Justina Vail

Law of Attraction – Michael Losier

Make Acting Work – Chrys Salt

Outliers – Malcolm Gladwell

The Artist's Way – Julia Cameron

The Biology of Belief – Bruce Lipton

The Happiness Advantage – Shawn Achor

The Secret – Rhonda Byrne

The Seven Habits of Highly Effective People – Stephen R. Covey

The Slight Edge – Jeff Olson

The Tao of Show Business – Dallas Travers

Think and Grow Rich – Napoleon Hill

Tipping Point – Malcolm Gladwell

War of Art – Steven Pressfield

You are the Placebo – Dr Joe Dispenza

You Were Born Rich – Bob Proctor

Printed in Poland
by Amazon Fulfillment
Poland Sp. z o.o., Wrocław